LOTS OF THANKS TO

My family members for their support

Tom Campbell (physicist/author of My Big TOE) for his truly awesome enlightenment

Chandler Bolt for sharing the following invaluable insight,

"Done is better than perfect'

Cheers matey!!!

My editor Masumi Atul Parmar

Moagi Lacoste Moiloanyane

Contents Page

INTRODUCTION

When it comes to the time for creating the specific personalities or characters for your book, you might find it a bit difficult. Unless you have an innate ability to imagine every aspect of each character at will, like most writers, you will turn to whatever sound advice you can get from books and online. What you usually end up with is a list of personality elements under each of which you will choose a list of attributes. Then further development is meant to be achieved throughout your storyline. This later evolution of a character includes using tips on how to bring their personality alive during the scenes. You hope that the actor will portray your theme and will delight and entertain the reader. Making the book a memorable experience is your primary goal. You could call this approach to character creation the 'Traditional Approach.'

This usual approach to character creation does work to some extent in the development of your characters, but it does not endow you, the writer, with a deep understanding of them. You begin to write your storyline with only some information about a character's outer identity, and hardly any knowledge of their inner personality. This blindness to your character's personality takes root when you are initially assigning some superficial psychological attributes to him. So, you do not know what your character's genuine reactions and behaviour should be because you have no solid reference points. You then find yourself randomly creating his or her psychology as you move through the storyline. But this chancing of your arm with a character's development during your storyline can lead to lots of inconsistencies, to loss of logical flow, along with loss of focus on the theme he represents. If you do manage to spot these errors within your storyline, you might eventually be left facing the dreaded scenario of having to stop and to begin again. At this point, your motivation can dry up as you become frustrated and begin to have self-doubts about ever writing your book. You are suddenly overwhelmed with a seemingly unresolvable problem. Ultimately this whole problem started at the character creation stage and specifically at the time you were assigning psychological attributes. The problem only makes itself known after you have started to write. The root of that problem is as follows:

> During the character creation stage, you did not
> create inner psychology for each character.

In this book, using an alternative approach, I am going to show you how to create character psychology rapidly, or in other words, to create the inner-self of a character. Unlike the traditional method which begins from outside of a character and works inwards, the alternative approach has the starting point on the inside with core psychology, and working outwards, developing motivations, values, emotional states, reactions, and perspective or outlook from that core.

By creating and having a psychological core for each character, you will have that solid reference point. You will continue to maintain an overview of the WHYs of each character's behaviour at every turn as you move through your storyline, and you can easily avoid those traditional pitfalls.

Following eight years of making it my sole mission to carry out an alternative study of the WHYs of behaviour, and after making thousands of notes, I arrived at ten solid and undeniable truths that underly behaviour in any given situation. To carry out this study, I used a simple method called 'Chain of Events.' To put it simply, a chain of events is a series of smaller events occurring within one chain leading to action on the part of a character.

For example:

(Event 1): An individual sees an advertisement for a cheeseburger

(Event 2): They suddenly feel hungry

(Event 3): A few minutes later, they are eating something.

That series of three events above are visible and not so difficult to work out because they begin at the conscious level of the individual's mind, work inwards, and then outwards. But there is a multitude of 'chains of events' occurring within the conscious and unconscious mind of an individual at any given moment, stretching both inwards and outwards and can begin with such things as memories, associations, imaginings, unconscious motivations, or very conscious emotions.

It was the understanding of these chains of events that eventually led me to deeper levels within an individual's mind, and it appears we all have a common core of truths, including different awareness levels in them, from which springs the potential for an infinite variety of behaviours. These core truths are the first events in any chain of events that occur within an individual's mind, and once you understand them, you can begin to have some understanding of the WHYs of behaviour. You can take this same understanding of the WHYs of behaviour from real life and bring it into the area of fictional character creation.

This understanding of the WHYs of behaviour or the chain of events within a character's mind is key to creating authentic and original characters. You can begin organising and developing a character's personality with that same deep core of truths and working outwards; you can create chains of events that lead to valid reasons for his or her behaviour within your storyline. Overall, you end up with a working holistic understanding of each character.

With this alternative approach to character creation, you suddenly find yourself possessing the ability to create specific characters for your themes and storyline. You will understand every aspect of a character entirely because you get to create each in their minutest details, details which will help you to bring them alive within your storyline. You get to create the usually hidden and unseen side of a character which ultimately drives behaviour. Finally, you know the WHYs of his or her behaviour at every turn within your storyline. Knowing your characters' psychology during your storyline in such depth will help in the generation of potential storylines for your book as well.

As the old saying goes, 'The proof is in the pudding.' The alternative approach to character creation, as shown in this book, is the same planned approach I used to write this book and will continue to apply to write the next and whatever follows. You are in the act of reading the proof you need that this new proposed approach surely works.

My promise to you is this: If you follow the alternative character creation steps as shown throughout this book, you will see amazing results in how you understand your characters throughout your storylines. In turn, this more profound conception allows for new creative expression with them.

If what I have said above defines some of your needs as a creative writer, then now is the right time to do something about fulfilling those requirements. Now is not the time to remain in the dark about the alternative character creation process presented in this book. Take this opportunity and gain a considerable advantage over the traditional approach. Avoid the usual pitfalls that could bring failure to all your hard work. Be one of those people who take an unusual and alternative approach to their goals, because these are usually the kind of people who are incredibly successful in what they set out to achieve.

While this book and its unique approach to character creation is the primary goal, there is something else that I am sure will intrigue you. As you move through the book, you will begin to see your reflection within the positive core of truths you will be using in the creation of your characters. There is a high probability that your self-evaluation will change to a more positive one. This book turns out to be, not only an excellent opportunity to learn a new holistic approach to character creation but doubles up to be also a journey of discovery into your inner-self, especially into those hidden realms of your creative imagination.

CHAPTER 1

THE TWO SELVES

'Most persons are so absorbed in the contemplation of

the outside world that they are wholly oblivious to

what is passing on within themselves.'

Nicola Tesla

Courtesy of: www.goalcast.com

Unlike the traditional approach to character creation where you create one whole character using just several character elements and attributes, the alternative method begins with two sides of a character – the inner-self and the outer-self. You then create the character from within to without.

Why the Division into Two Selves?

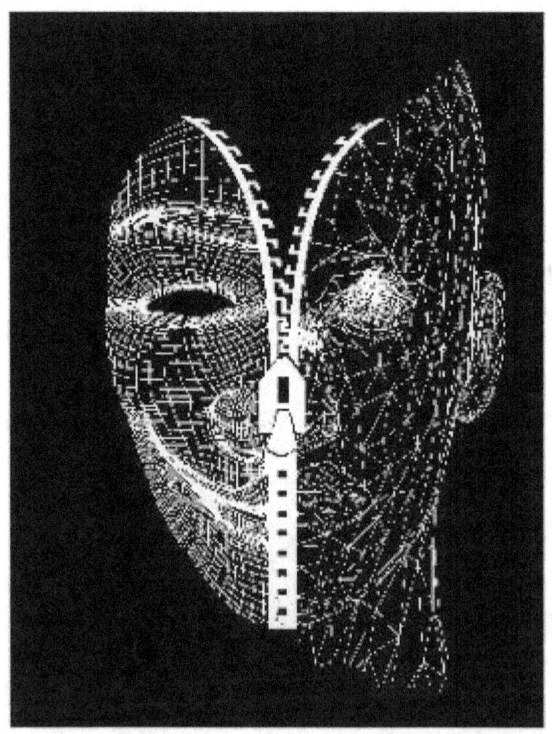

Two Selves Division: img 2

This division into two selves during the creation stage might appear to make the task of creating a character far more complicated and complex than it usually is. But, as you will see, it makes the process a lot simpler as well as giving you a continuous deep understanding of your characters throughout the storyline. Two simple sentences can sum up the basic plan for the creation process:

- o   You begin by creating the usually hidden and unseen inner-self of a character that drives his behaviour

- o   Then using your understanding of the character's deeper inner-self, it enables you to work outwards to create the outer-self

At the end of this character creation procedure, a whole new and original character emerges every time, ready to make their debut into your creative writing.

In other words, by beginning the creation of a character as two separate selves, it allows you to create both the inner core of the character's psychology and their outer behaviour as different parts. You then bring those two parts together as one whole.

Now you will know what his or her likely motivations, values, and behaviours will be in reaction to events and other characters within your storyline. You know in depth ahead of time what the WHYs of their action is, and what their reflexes will be. No more random creation and development of characters throughout the storyline is needed.

Once you understand the nature of the 'Two Selves' and how they form the whole character, you suddenly have the power and the ability to create the specific and authentic characters you need for your storyline and themes.

So, to repeat, initially, you must see both selves as separate and with different natures. Only then can you move on to understand how these two selves interact or come together to generate the WHYs of a character's behaviour.

This process of beginning with two separate selves will simplify as we go into each new chapter and your understanding of the two-selves approach to character creation deepens.

In the next chapter, I will show you the core attributes used to create the inner-self of a character.

CHAPTER 2

INNER-SELF TRUTHS

'But instinct is something which transcends knowledge. We have, undoubtedly,
certain finer fibres that enable us to perceive truths when logical deduction, or any
other willful effort of the brain, is futile.'

Nicola Tesla

Courtesy of: www.goalcast.com

Truths as Attributes

When thinking about creating a character, we usually think about character
attributes. But these traditional attributes are too shallow or superficial to capture the
true inner essence of a character. We need something with more depth than mere
attributes.

So rather than referring to attributes, we will refer to ten inner-self core truths.
Everything else about the character falls out of these truths.

The crucial point to understand about these truths during the character creation
stage is the awareness level you give to a character within each. The higher the
awareness level in each revelation, the better life will be for a character and vice
versa. In other words, every personality you create will have specific awareness
levels within a combination of truths leading to particular reactions and behaviour.

Have a look at the image below:

○ Purpose to Evolve	Others ○
○ Free-Will	Creativity ○
○ Love	All-Possibility ○
○ Wisdom	Immortality ○
○ Morality	Self-Identity ○

Ten Inner-Self Truths: img 3

The ten truths listed above make up the nature of a character's inner self. They are the ten inner-self truths that we start with when creating a character from scratch. There are some more truths we can use, but the ten shown above sufficiently cover the creation of a broad range of personalities. From the wise man to the psychopath, these ten truths include all possible behaviours needed for any character in any storyline.

One point I want to make clear here is that my definitions of a truth and truth awareness levels within a character are just that – my definitions.

Your definitions are just as valid as anyone else's. Feeling free with your character definitions is a must if you want your creative writing to flow.

Definition of a Truth

You can find many definitions of what truth is in books and online such as the following:

- o Truth is self-evident and is eternal.

But the above short definition does not provide useful insights into what truth is for our character creation purposes. To gain a more in-depth insight into what truth is, you must see it in action with other truths, or to understand the truth you must see how it influences other truths and how this combined influence underlies a character's behaviour.

For example: 'Purpose to Evolve' is one of the ten truths used in this book. If a character has no sense of purpose to evolve, then there will be little experience of hope. They will see the state of things as fixed and unchangeable. They will respond with self-survival interests with none of the other truths such as 'Others,' 'Love' or 'Wisdom' guiding that response. They will suffer as they make choices and take actions that are incompatible with their inner-self truths leading to the other characters suffering as well.

But if a character has an awareness of their purpose to evolve, they will have the light of hope within themselves. It will be possible to see the other truths such as 'All-Possibility,' 'Immortality,' and 'Creativity.' They will thrive in positive feelings leading to greater happiness for themselves and the other characters as well.

In the light of what I said above:

- o Truths are active and interactive dynamics within a character, and whether they are fully aware of them or not, will generate the basis of their perspective and behaviour.

For example, a character who is only aware of themselves as an isolated individual and knows nothing of the truth of their collective nature is likely to think, choose, and act in ways that inflame, causes anger, and pain in the other characters as they pursue self-survival.

Core Psychology

As I said in chapter one, it is crucial to begin creating your character on the inside, starting with the inner self. Have a look at the following points about these inner-self truths:

- o They form the core psychology of your character and play a significant role in their makeup, outlook, and behaviour

- o You can hardwire each character you create with these ten truths along with various levels of awareness in them. Their perspective, motivations, choice of values, emotional states, desires, wants, needs and actions will spring from them. In other words, their outer-self springs from them

Another area you need to consider when creating a character is the awareness level in those truths given. The three broad awareness levels are as follows:

- o A character will be completely unaware of their inner-self truths, and in their place, they will be interpreting their world with illusions and fictions. These illusions and fantasies lead to lots of errors.

- o They will have some awareness of their inner-self truths mixed with illusions and fictions.

- o They will be fully aware of their inner-self truths and will have no illusions and fictions

Assigning any one of these three quite distinct truth awareness levels to a character will mean striking differences between themselves and other characters. The following method will show you how to achieve those differences between characters.

Awareness Level Scale

To determine one of those three awareness levels for a character just mentioned above, you will be using what I call the 'Awareness Level Scale.'

In this section and using the scales, I will show you two brief examples of a character's possible awareness in two of the ten truths shown above. I will also show you how these different awareness levels translate to different outer-self behaviour.

We will take the truths of 'Creativity' and 'Morality' as our examples here. Have a look at the image below:

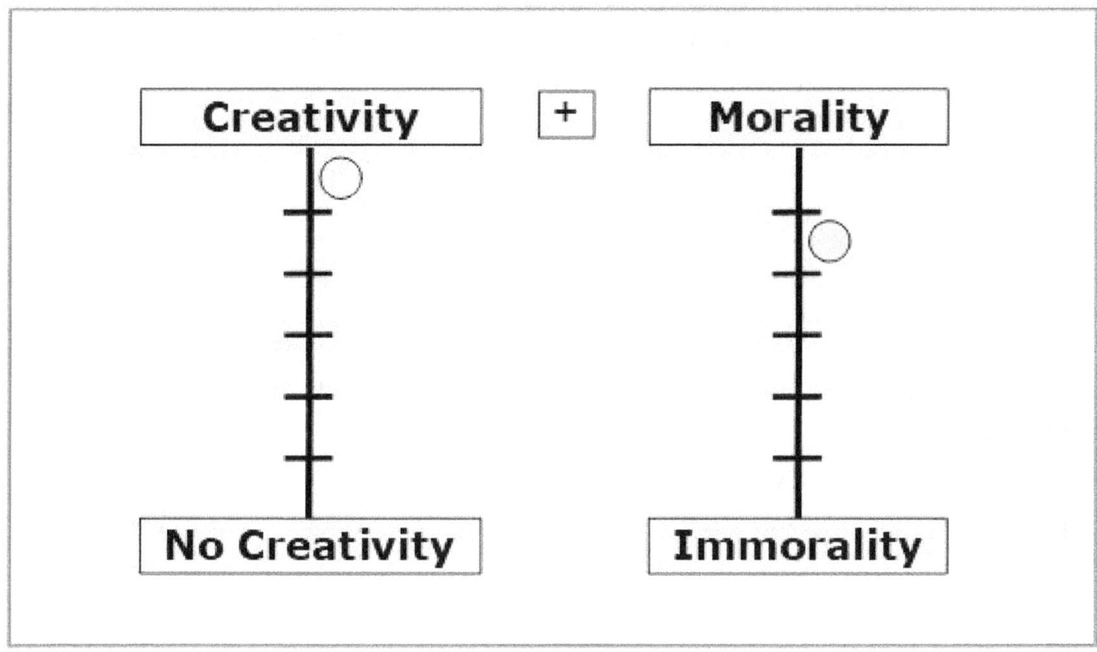

Awareness Level Scale: img 4

In the image above, I have placed both the truths of 'Creativity' and 'Morality into the Awareness Level Scale.

Making up the scales is a vertical pole divided into six levels. At the top is the name of the truth and at the bottom is its antonym.

You will also notice an indicator positioned within the scale for each truth. The higher the level of the gauge, the more awareness the character will have in that truth and vice versa.

During the creation stage, if you place an indicator at a high level for 'Creativity,' it means the character will have a strongly felt conscious need to be creative. This high level of creativity will translate to their motivations, into the choice of values made, and into behaviour. They will be highly creative in whatever field they choose. It's this translation from the core of truths to a character's behaviour is what you will learn to do in this book.

To go with this high level of creativity, if you also give a character a high level in 'Morality' as shown by the indicator in the image above, this deeply felt sense of what is right will guide them in their creations. They will create things that are beneficial and valuable to both themselves and others.

But because a character has a high level of awareness in creativity, it does not mean they will be of benefit to themselves and others.

Have a look at the following image:

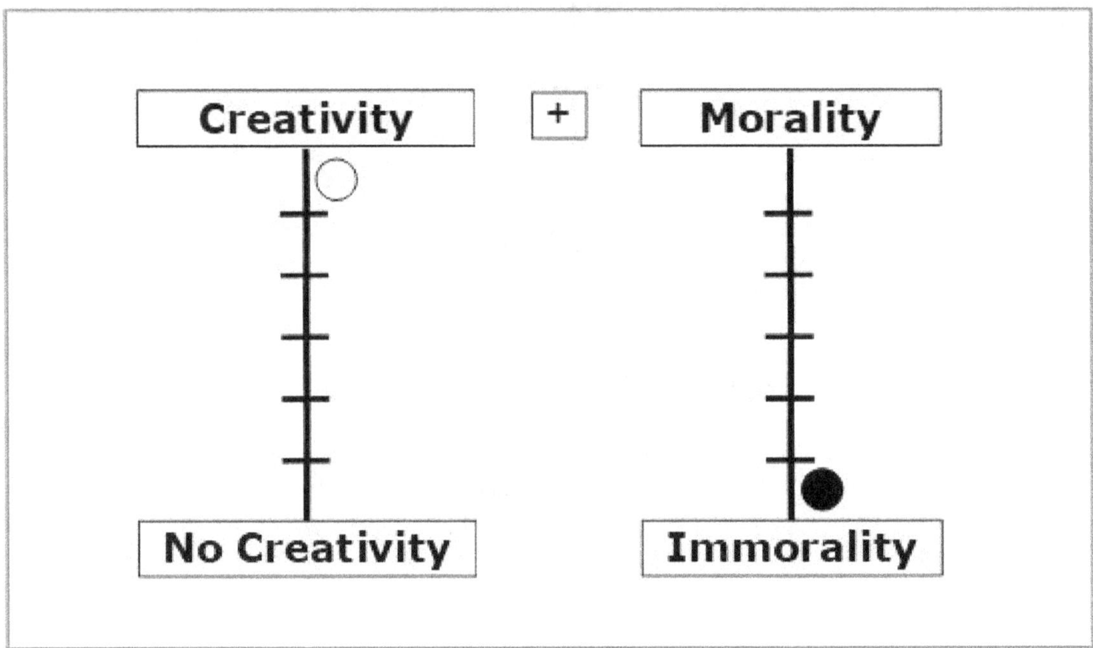

Awareness Level Scale: img 5

In the image above, we have the same two truths of 'Creativity' and 'Morality.' But this time there is a clear difference. The high level of creativity assigned to the character remains, but now a low level for morality has been given.

The character will still have a strong urge and ability to be creative, but this time they will have no moral sense guiding them in their creative activity. With this specific level of awareness, chances are, they will create things that will appear to be beneficial and rewarding to themselves, but at the same time will be directly harmful and threatening to others in many ways.

The two examples above clearly reveal how the awareness levels between truths interact to generate a character's behaviour. Remember, there are ten core truths and those two examples above only revealed the cause and effect between two of those truths. As soon as you have created a character using combinations of truths and their specific awareness levels, you will be able to see the WHYs of their behaviour throughout your storyline.

Creating Differences in Characters

You can also use the Awareness Level Scale to create vast differences between characters during the character creation stage. These differences created at the level of the truth will translate to different motivations that project outwards into entirely different choices of values and behaviours for each of the characters.

In other words, by giving different awareness levels to several truths for each character, guarantees original characters who are distinctive from each other at the psychological core level. It then follows that the behaviour of the characters will be diverse as well.

Knowing all the awareness levels in each truth within a given character will give you the bigger picture of the WHYs of their behaviour. You will know their strengths and weaknesses, and this will help you to avoid being inconsistent in what you write about the character.

Character Change

One of the central truths of the inner self is 'Purpose to Evolve.' You might need a character to change for the better as your storyline progresses, and this change occurs when the levels of awareness in inner-self truths begin to move up to higher levels. When this happens, they suddenly have access to higher levels of knowledge and awareness, and their behaviour within your storyline will change for the better. For example, they will be more emotionally positive. You can then base those changes for the better within the character's actions and behaviour.

But all good storylines need a character to devolve at some point. To devolve means that some of the awareness levels you initially assigned to them during the creation stage have begun to move down the scales, especially when it comes to the awareness level in 'Morality.' This character will become more emotionally harmful to themselves and others.

In either case above, at any point or turn of events during the storyline, you can go back to a character's initial truth profile and make those changes in their awareness levels. From there, you can then identify their new motivations, their different choice of values, their emotional reactions, and their future actions.

Character Flaws and Errors

During the character creation stage, if you were to position the indicator within all inner-self truths at their highest levels of awareness for a character – remember, there are ten inner-self truths - that character's purpose to evolve would be complete. You would then have a saint, a spiritual man, a Buddha, or an extremely enlightened being. This perfection and the highest level of awareness in all truths is the goal of the inner-self purpose to evolve. The character would have no flaws or errors in their behaviour.

But as we all know, most characters need their flaws and errors to make the storyline exciting for the reader. You create the potential for these flaws and errors within a character by assigning low levels of awareness within their core of truths.

Before we move onto the character creation stage in chapter four, let us have a more detailed look at the Awareness Level Scale.

CHAPTER 3

AWARENESS LEVEL SCALE

'Although it is difficult to pinpoint the physical base or location of awareness, it is perhaps the most precious thing concealed within our brains. And it is something that the individual alone can feel and experience. Each of us cherishes it highly, yet it is private.'

Dalai Lama

Courtesy of: www.JuicyQuotes.com

The biggest problem to overcome for any writer of books or plays that require a range of different characters is knowing what kind of awareness each character should have and will bring to the storyline. A writer should make efforts to create a specific level of knowledge or appreciation in those truths for each character, and this, in turn, also helps to create the differences between the characters. It is from this understanding that a writer can maintain the differences between characters.

But before you can create a specific awareness level for a character, there are a couple of questions to be asked.

Character Creation Questions

One of the toughest parts of creating a character for your storyline and themes of your book is to find a starting point. In pursuit of this starting point, the following type of questions will be going through your mind:

- o Where do I begin?

- o What do I know about my character's psychology?

- o What do I know about their motivations?

- o Which values will I assign to them?

o   What will be their emotional reactions and behaviour?

o   How do I justify what I write about them?

o   Can I gain consistency in what I write about a character throughout my storyline?

o   Will the character be authentic and believable for the reader?

Those are just some of the questions that can spark off writer's panic if you wait to create a character's inner psychology during your storyline. You are left sitting there wondering what to write, with no inspiration coming, or you might just write something about the character that is incompatible with what you wrote earlier about them. Either way, it does not work out as you would have preferred. You then find yourself deleting large chunks of text or balling-up pages of hard work and throwing them into the wastebasket.

The problem occurs because you are mostly outside of the character's mind or perspective, or more to the point, you do not know or understand their core psychology because you have not made an effort to create one for them.

The alternative approach to character creation used in this book puts you directly inside the character's mind at a character's creation stage and provides you with that elusive starting point. From this starting point, you will be creating characters from the inside and working outwards using the Awareness Level Scale.

From the very beginnings of a character's creation, you are in there creating the deepest crevices of their mind, and your presence in there will continue throughout your book, in every sentence you write.

With the Awareness Level Scale, you are a character's creator before they make their debut into your storyline, the director of their behaviour during the action and events while knowing their destiny and their fate from the word go.

The Awareness Level Scale gives you those advantages and more.

Awareness Level Scale

The Awareness Level Scale is beneficial during the character creation stage. It helps you to overcome many of the obstacles you would typically face.

Have a look at the following image:

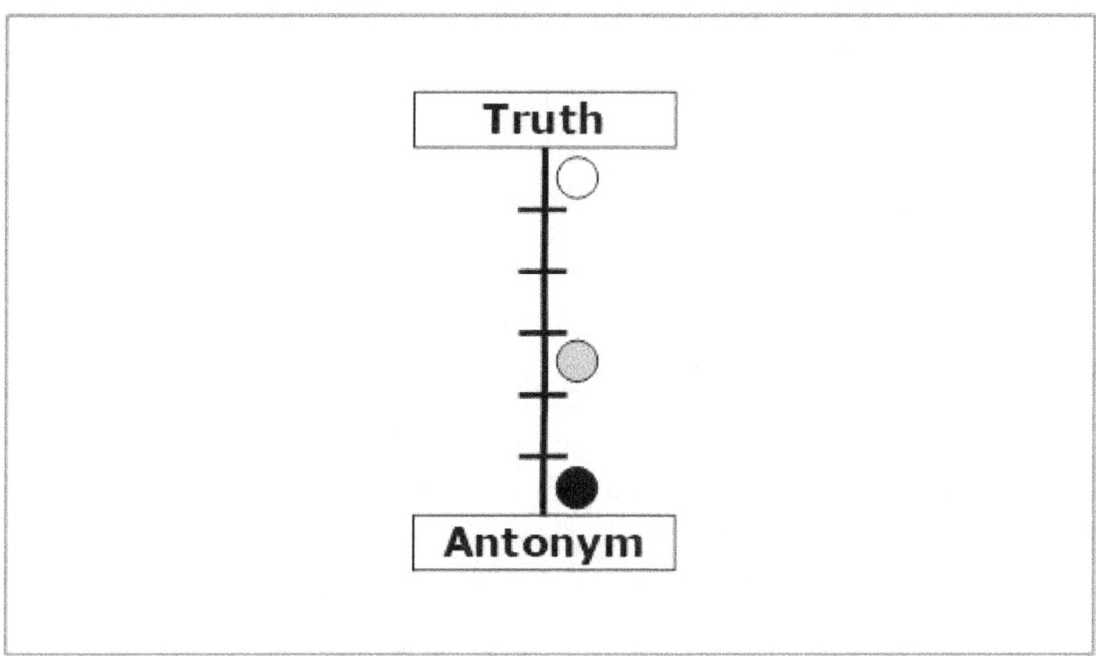

Awareness Level Scale: img 6

As I said in the last chapter, making up the Awareness Level Scale is a vertical pole containing six different levels. Each level represents different levels of awareness or non-awareness of truth within your character's conscious mind.

At the top of the pole, you place the name of the specific truth you are using during your character creation stage, and at the bottom of the pole, you set the antonym of that truth.

To assign a higher level of awareness in truth, you place a grey or white indicator on one of the levels above the centre of the scales. The higher the level, the more awareness a character will have in the given truth, and the more positive the emotions will be. The choice of specific awareness levels in truth will translate out to different motivations, choices of values, and behaviour by the character.

To assign a lack of awareness in truth, you place a grey or black indictor on one of the levels below the centre of the scales towards the truth's antonym. The lower the level, the less awareness in the given truth and the more negative the emotions will be. Again, the chosen level of awareness will translate out to different motivations, choices of values, and behaviour for the character.

As we saw in chapter two with 'Creativity' and 'Morality,' a character can also be assigned a high level of awareness in one truth, and a lack of awareness in another. A change in motivations, chosen values, and behaviour will follow.

Positive and Negative Emotions

Positioning a white indicator at the highest level in the scales for a given truth will mean the character will have mainly positive emotions.

The grey indicator shows that the character will have a mix of negative and positive emotions due to their semi-awareness of the truth.

A black indicator shows that the character has no awareness for that truth and is extremely likely to be full of hatreds and other negativities.

The white, grey, and black indicators will also point to the type of motivations, choice of values, desires, needs, wants, and behaviour a character will have.

Levels on the Scale

The levels above the centre line of the scales represent the inner-self truth awareness level of a character. In contrast, the levels below the centre line of the scales represent the outer-self unawareness of a truth. Awareness or unawareness of truth ultimately finds its way into a character's interpretation and understanding of events. These interpretations are earlier events in the chain of logic that lead to the later developments in that chain, such as emotional responses and actions taken.

In other words, a character who has white or light grey indicators placed above the centre line has both inner-self and outer-self focus. This awareness level becomes the character's guide in shaping interpretations and understanding of events.

In contrast, a character having a dark grey and or black indicator below the centre line will be only aware of their outer-self. There is little or no awareness of their inner-self truths, and so no insight from these truths which in turn, don't underpin their interpretations and understanding. Their final actions are always missing this vital meaning or information.

As you will see further on, those inner-self or outer-self focuses referred to above have vast implications for a character in their outer-self world or the world that you write for them.

One more vital point to make is that you do not necessarily need more than a combination of two or three truths and awareness levels in them for any one character. This combination of two or three truths will be active or nonactive within a character leading to specific motivations, values, and behaviour. Again, this is another way of creating apparent differences between your characters.

Let us take another look at what was said above again, just in different words.

Awareness Level Scale and the Outer-Self

During the character creation stage, whenever you place an indicator on a level below the centre line of the pole for a given truth, you are giving the character an outer-self focus, and they will lack the awareness and insights of the specific truth in question. They will only have the information on their outer world to interpret and understand their experiences.

Outer-Self Motivations and Values

A character with an indicator below the centre line of the pole will find their motivations and their values solely from the outer-self world.

Outer-Self Emotions and Behaviour

The level of placement of an indicator within the scales will determine the nature of the character's emotions and behaviour. An indicator placed at a level below the centre line will have negative feelings. The further down the scales for the indicator, the more negative are their emotions. So, during the character creation stage, the levels within the pole are not only a way of setting up a character's motivations and values, but also a way of setting up the character's emotional states and their kneejerk responses. They will react with these emotions and with the behaviour that accompanies them within your storyline.

Awareness Level Scale and the Inner-Self

During the character creation stage, whenever you place an indicator on a level above the centre line of the pole for a given truth, you are giving the character a level of inner-self focus, and they will be aware of that truth to some degree. They will have the insights of the given truth to aid them in their interpretations and understanding of their experiences.

Inner-Self Motivations and Values

A character with an indicator above the centre line of the pole will find their motivations and values mainly from their inner-self world. However, they will find some positive motivations and values in their outer-self world as well.

Inner-Self Emotions and Behaviour

As I said above, the level of placement of an indicator within the scales will determine the nature of the character's emotions and behaviour. An indicator placed at a level above the centre line will have positive feelings. The further up the scales for the indicator, the more favourable are their emotions. They will express these emotions and the behaviour that accompanies them within your storyline.

Practice

A great way to learn this alternative character creation process is to put in some practice in the following way:

(1) Begin by selecting one truth and one awareness level for that truth. Let a theme you might want to write about determine which truth to select. Just write some quick paragraphs to get the ideas flowing.

(2) Now try to identify and to create a profile list of a character's likely motivations, chosen values, emotions and behaviour based on that truth and its given awareness level.

(3) Begin again, but this time select a different awareness level for the same truth. Repeat the cycle.

(4) Your next step might be to add a second truth and an awareness level for that. Again, see if you can identify a character's likely behaviour from the interaction of the selected truths. Repeat the cycle. Go as far as you can until it gets too complicated to calculate the character's likely behaviour..

Practising will help you to see why I suggested only using two or three truths and given awareness levels for each character. The more truths you use, the more complicated it gets to identify likely behaviour.

Final Notes

It is the understanding of this infinite potential and possibility of combinations of core inner-self truths and their selected awareness levels that will allow you to create original and authentic characters every time before you sit down to write your novel or play.

The following chapters show you how to project a character's likely motivations, values, emotions, and behaviour from these inner-self truths and antonyms.

CHAPTER 4

TRUTHS AND OUTER-SELF VALUES

'PURPOSE TO EVOLVE'

'A life is never useless. Each soul that came down to earth is here for a reason.'

Paulo Coelho

Courtesy of: www.brainquotes.org

The Goal of this Chapter

In this chapter, I will explain the first of the ten inner-self truths to show you how to translate it to a character's outer-self values and behaviour. I will be referring to a character as they/them.

But firstly, let us go over a summary of the steps you will take to create a character.

Matching Truths to Values

There are four necessary steps you will take to create a character.

- o Decide on which side of a theme the character you are about to create will be representing. An argument has two sides, such as 'Truth versus Deception' or 'Others versus Individuality.'

- o Then you select the truths and the awareness levels within them that go with the theme.

- o You then select a list of social values or external motivations the character will be attracted to. It is at this point, you can add the traditional character elements and attributes.

- o Then work the character into your storyline based on your developed understanding of them.

Each time you complete one of those four steps above, the information pulled together for that step will automatically suggest the information for the next level.

So, let us begin with the first of the ten truths – 'Purpose to Evolve.'

Truth 1 - Purpose to Evolve

'Purpose to Evolve' means that a character will feel the need to become more in empathy, in compassion, in love, in wisdom than they are at present. They will desire to become more than they are, to rise to the highest level of awareness within all their inner-self truths.

Have a look at the following image:

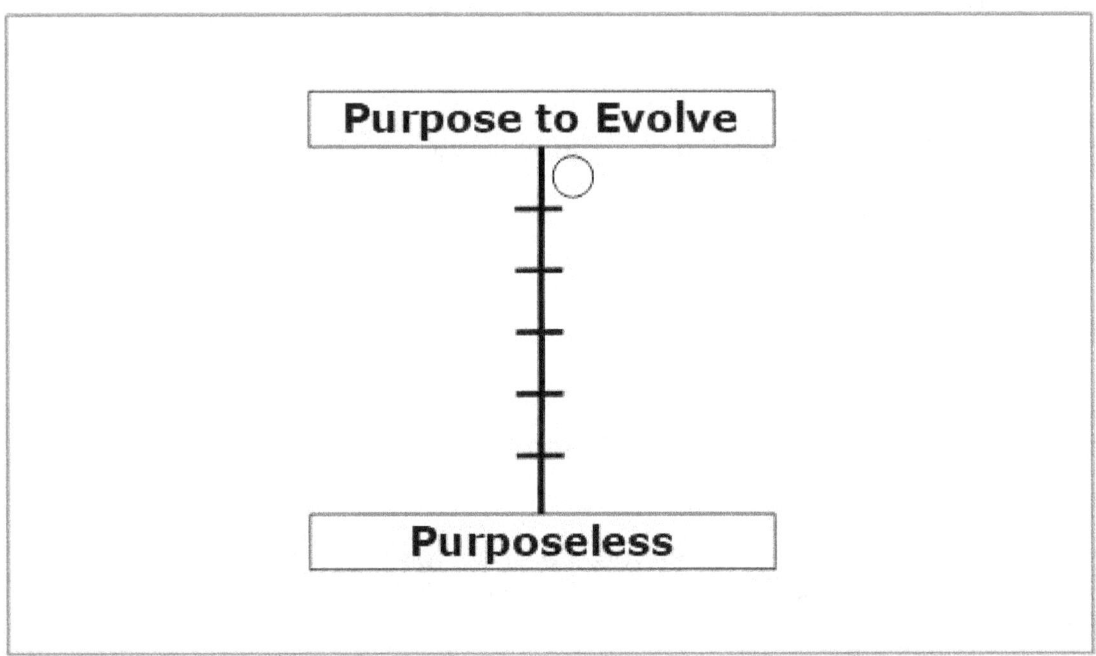

Awareness Level Scale: img 7

Assigning a High Level of Awareness

When you are creating a character, if you give them the highest level of awareness for their inner-self purpose to evolve, this will mean you have given them a drive towards specific outer-self values. This inner drive becomes their internal motivation.

Now you need to translate this inner motivation across to their outer-self motives. In this book, those outer-self motivations are what the character considers as values. These values are usually social values.

Values and Motivations

A character with a high level of awareness in their purpose to evolve will have the following motivations or values:

- o   Continually observing and changing themselves for the better

- o   Continually attempting to reform society

- o   Trying to bring progressive changes to the broader world

These are only some broad examples of the social values a character might have if you give them the highest awareness level in their 'Purpose to Evolve.' You can add many more outer-self values to that list.

If one of your themes is 'Change versus Tradition' or something similar, then you will need a character who will have these types of motivations or values to champion that cause within your storyline. This character will represent change.

Emotional States

A character with a high level of awareness in their 'Purpose to Evolve' will find lots of fulfilment in their successes and will experience positive feelings, rarely feeling negative, even in the face of challenges, obstacles, and failures.

Chain of Events for this Character

In the case of the given character above, the chain of events in the way they see things is as follows:

- o   They are connected to the truths of their inner-self and can see the true purpose to life

- o The action of the truth 'Purpose to Evolve' influences their conscious mind

- o They experience this 'Purpose to Evolve' influence as inner motivation

- o They are attracted to specific social values or motivations in their outer-self world

- o They make choices and take actions, also based on their outer-self values.

- o They will tend to have positive emotional responses.

Assigning a Low Level of Awareness

Have a look at the image below:

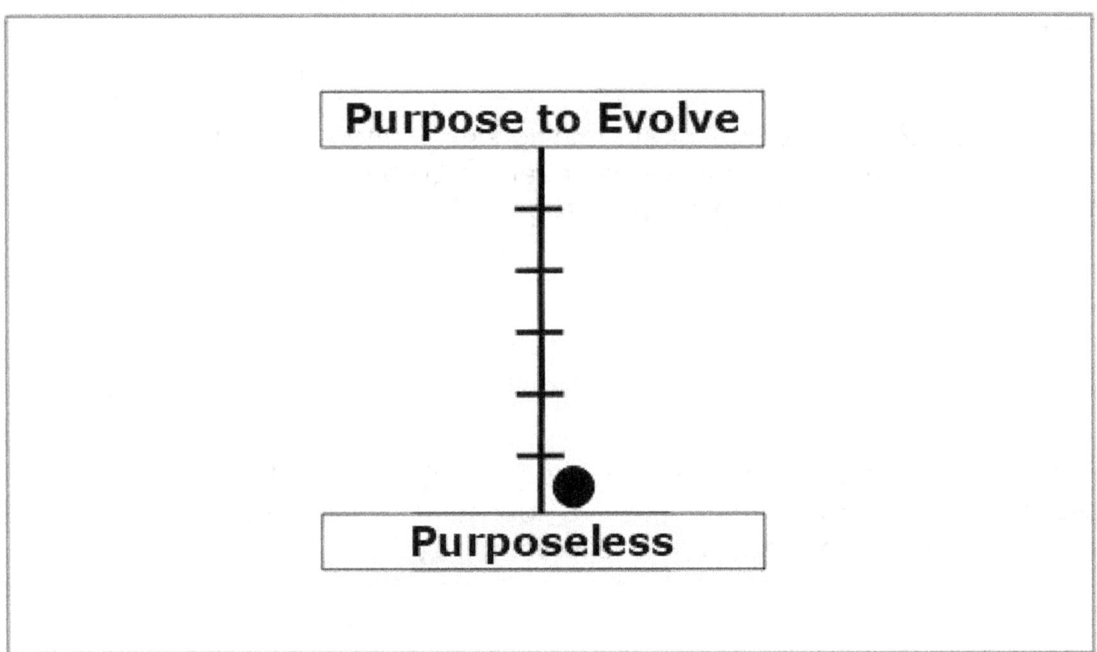

Awareness Level Scale: img 8

But a character can also be given a low awareness level for their 'Purpose to Evolve.'

The character's conscious outer-self will be utterly blind to their inner-self purpose to evolve, will probably find life to be pointless, and will wonder what it is all about.

They will attempt to fill this void within themselves with outer-self purposes, and usually with goals that are in direct conflict, or not compatible with their inner-self purpose to evolve.

Values and Motivations

With no awareness of their real purpose to evolve, the character will likely fill the void with the following social values as an end in itself:

- Money, power, wealth

- Be motivated only to possess things for themselves

- Has a drive only for self-consumption with little consideration for others

Those are only a few broad examples. You can add many more outer motivations to that list above.

This character can represent the 'Tradition' side of your theme of 'Change versus Tradition' within your storyline because they are highly likely to fall in with whatever values their society holds, even if those values seem fair but are unjust and unfair.

Remember, you are matching up awareness
levels within a character's inner-self truths to both
the possible values he will have and to his behaviour.

Emotional States

This character will be full of negative emotions, tends to blame others, and the world if they don't get what they want.

You can get lists of unacceptable behaviour, antisocial behaviour or criminal behaviour online to assign to your character during their creation stage.

Chain of Events for this Character

In the case of the given character above, the chain of events in the way they see things is as follows:

- They have lost contact with the truths of their inner-self and can see no real purpose to life

- Because they are blind to their real purpose to evolve, they look to outer motivations to fill the void

- Their choices and actions are solely based on this outer motivation

- They will continually have extremely negative emotional responses.

CHAPTER 5

TRUTHS AND OUTER-SELF VALUES

'FREE-WILL'

'I must be willing to give up what I am now, in order to become what I will be.'

Albert Einstein

Courtesy of: quotefancy

The Goal of this Chapter

In this chapter, I will be going through the second of the ten truths - 'Free Will' - to show you how to translate it to a character's outer-self values and behaviour.

But firstly, lets again run over the four necessary steps you will take to create a character.

Matching Truths to Values

There are four necessary steps you will take:

- o   Decide on which side of a theme the character will be representing.

- o   Select the truths and the awareness level within them a character would most likely have or not have for the theme.

- o   Select a list of social values and external motivations the character will find attractive.

- o   Work the character into your storyline based on the above understanding.

Truth 2 – Free-Will

Our second inner-self truth is 'Free-Will.' It is directly related to the first truth – 'Purpose to Evolve' – in that, a character is free to make choices and to take actions that will either aid their growth or cause them to go into a decline. In other words, their decisions and actions will either be good or bad for themselves and others. All inner-self truths are interrelated like this.

Assigning a High Level of Awareness

Some characters will be highly aware of the power of their free-will in all situations and of how their free-will choices and actions will affect themselves and others.

Have a look at the following image:

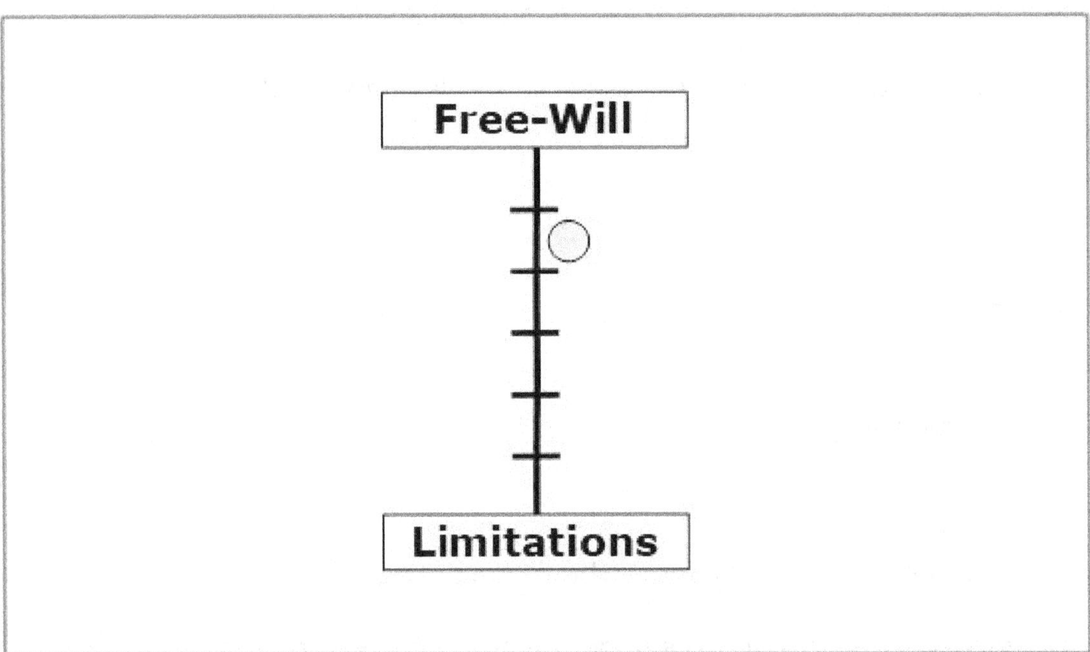

Awareness Level Scale: img 9

In the image above, I have assigned a high level of awareness in free-will to the character.

But having free-will by itself does not guarantee that a character will always make the right choices and take the right actions. Thought alone does not suffice. We need something else as guidance. That something else is another truth.

Have a look at the following image:

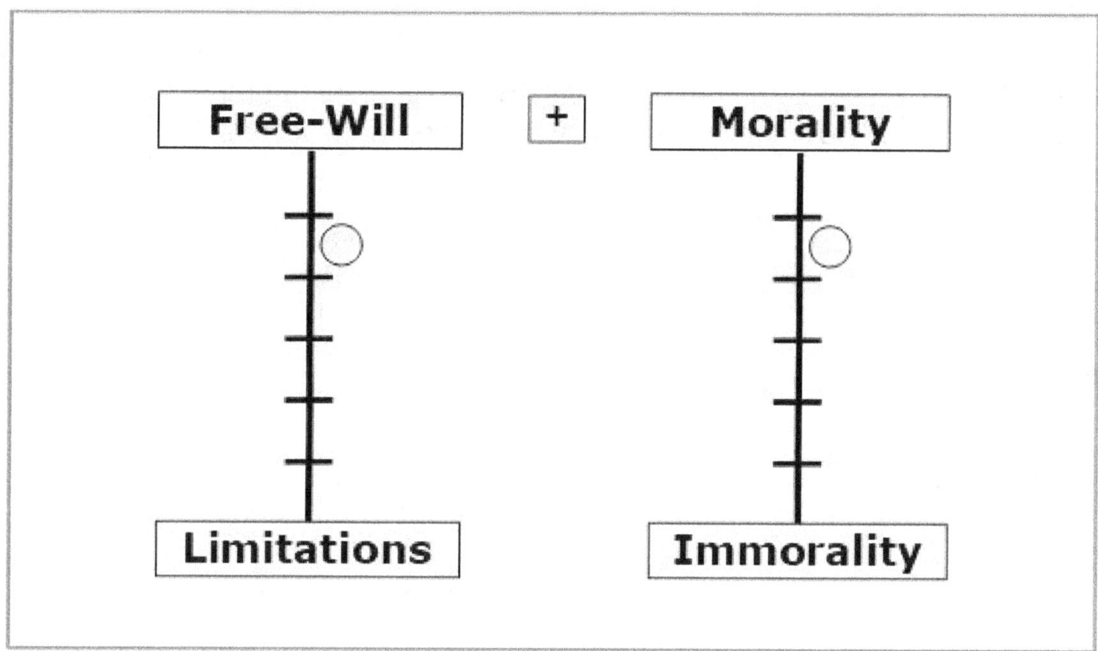

Awareness Level Scale: img 10

In the image above, I have added a second truth along with its awareness level for the character. Adding several truths together is what you do when creating a character. You combine two or three of them along with selected awareness levels in them. Then you make the influence of these combined truths determine the character's motivations, chosen values, and behaviour. The theme the character is to represent will decide which combination of truths and awareness levels you will need for that character.

In the case above, the character's high sense of morality will guide them in their free-will choices and actions.

Remember, all ten truths are interrelated and influence each other before projecting out as the character's overall behaviour.

No Limitations

Another factor in free-will is the perception of limitations characters will have on themselves. The character above will have learned that good free-will choices do not limit in any way.

If you need a conscientious character for your storyline, you will give them a high level of awareness in both free-will and morality.

This character will always attempt to stay on the right path because their moral sense gives them an understanding of how their own free-will choices and actions affect themself and others.

Values and Motivations

A character having a conscious awareness of their free-will combined with a heightened sense of morality will have the following type of values and motivations as follows:

- Careful with how they think
- Careful with the choices they make
- Careful to take the right actions
- Will be mindful of others in everything they decide and do
- Will have a heightened sense of duty and responsibility
- Will have accountability
- Will be conscientiousness

Those are only a few examples of the power of conscious free-will being influenced by a high sense of morality.

If you need a character to represent a theme within your storyline such as 'Responsibility versus Negligence' then you would give them those high levels of awareness in both free-will and morality to champion the 'Responsibility' side of the theme.

Emotional States

This character will derive great satisfaction and positiveness from freely fulfilling their sense of moral duty. You can look up 'positive emotions lists' online or get them from a thesaurus.

Chain of Events for this Character

In the case of the given character above, the chain of events in the way they see things is as follows:

- They are connected to the truths of their inner-self and can see the true meaning to life

- The combined action of both truths, 'Free-Will' and 'Morality" influences their conscious mind

- They experience this influence as their inner motivation

- They are attracted to specific social values or outer motivations in their outer-self world

- They make choices and take actions, also based on their outer-self values.

- They will tend to have positive emotional responses and will experience a lot of satisfaction

Assigning a Low Level of Awareness

Have a look at the image below:

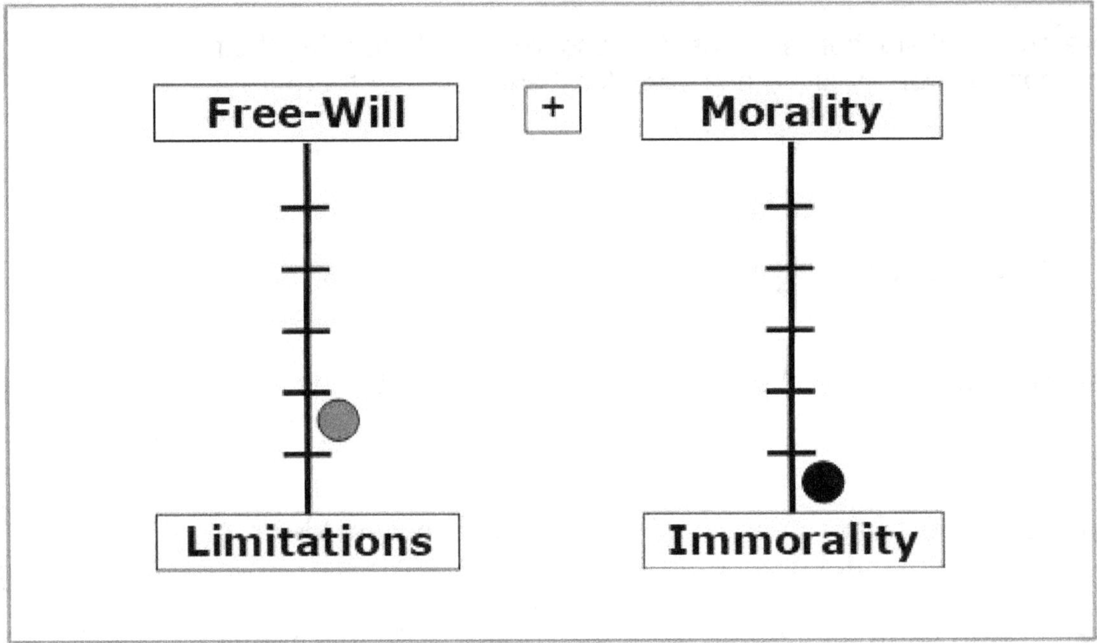

Awareness Level Scale: img 11

But a character can be given a low awareness level for both 'Free-Will' and 'Morality.'

One of your themes might be 'Power and Corruption', and so you will need an unconscientious or questionable character, maybe holding a high office or post in their society to represent the corruption side of the theme.

Values and Motivations

- Power and influence

- Wealth

- Yachts, big houses, fancy cars, jewellery

- Anything else that gives them satisfaction

Wanting those values does not make them corrupt, but when a character has no sense of morality, they will act in the following way in pursuit of their personal goals:

- o Neglectful of their moral obligation to others

- o In violation of expected codes of conduct

- o Evasive

- o Corrupt

- o Unscrupulous

- o Spends a lot of time covering their tracks

- o Can be a charmer but with hidden motives

- o Can be violent when others get in their way

Again, those are only a few examples of limited free-will combined with a lack of moral sense.

When creating this corrupt character, you can assign those negative motivations to them because they have no moral sense or have lost sight of their moral sense in pursuit of outer-self ambitions and values.

Limitations

Also remember, that a character who acts in those ways above sees the lack of power, wealth, and influence as limitations on them, and so they will do anything in their power to possess them. They limit their free-will in pursuit of those outer values.

Emotional States

Look up some emotional lists online and select a few of the nastier negative emotions. Assign these to this character as the likely reactions to others within your storyline.

Chain of Events for this Character

In the case of the given character above, the chain of events in the way they see things is as follows:

- They have lost contact with the truths of their inner-self and can see no real meaning to life

- Believe their free-will can only be focused outwards at the objects and values of society

- Think they will have their freedom if they manage to possess those objects and values

- Will stop at nothing in pursuit of their ambitions

- In the process, they leave a trail of misery for others behind them

- No matter how much they do manage to obtain, they can never be happy and always wants more

CHAPTER 6

TRUTHS AND OUTER-SELF VALUES

'WISDOM'

'The greatest of all pleasures is the pleasure of learning.'

Aristotle

Courtesy of: Quote Finder

Truth 3 - Wisdom

Our third truth is 'Wisdom.' Wisdom involves having deep insights and understanding of truths that guide and shape behaviour.

Assigning a High Level of Awareness

Have a look at the following image:

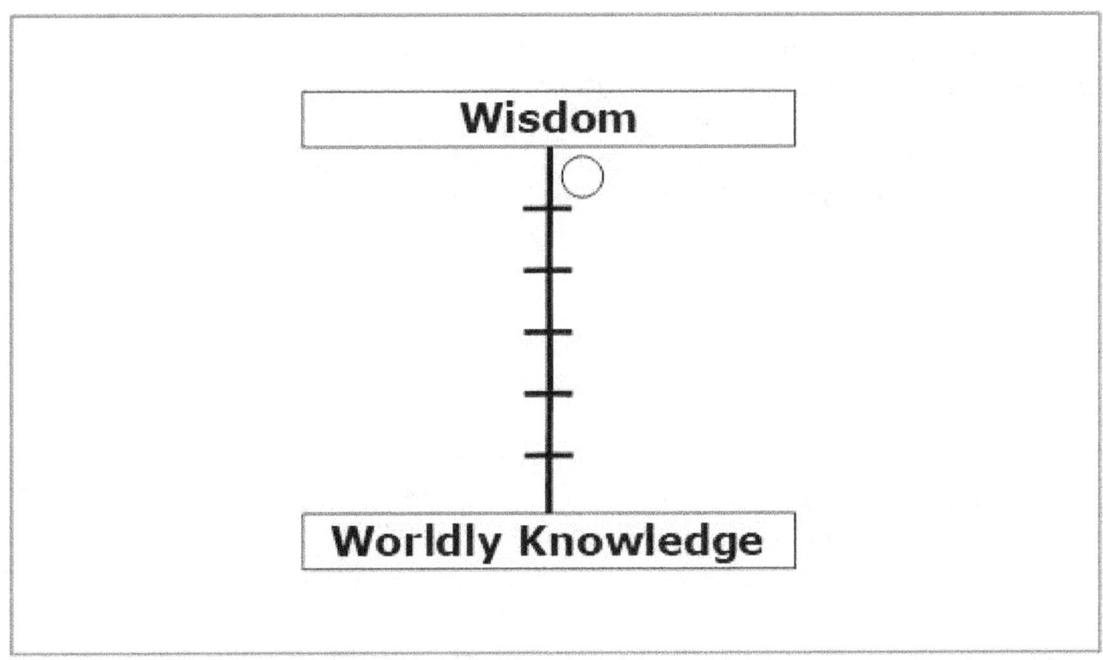

Awareness Level Scale: img 12

During the character creation stage, if you decide to assign the highest awareness level in 'Wisdom', this means the character will possess an elevated awareness and understanding in all ten truths.

They will enter your storyline with a deep understanding of their inner-self nature, of their purpose to evolve, and of their need to grow in love and empathy.

Motivations

This character's exalted inner-self knowledge and understanding will guide their behaviour in the following way:

- o They will have a higher level of awareness than the other characters

- o Will be humble, silent, but brilliant

- o Will be moderate, temperate, and disciplined

- o Will be able to visualise workable solutions

- o Their focus will be on their curiosity and discovery

- o They will show deep understanding, knowledge, learning, and insightfulness in everything they say, write or do

If you need a character like this for one of your themes, then you would assign these types of inner motivations to them when you are creating them.

In their wisdom, this character will probably live alone and in isolation with the bare essentials in life, and not bother with the accumulation of worldly social values.

Values

During their solitude, they will more than likely be recording their contemplations and insights. Eventually, and usually after the death of the wise character, someone discovers their notes and compiles a book. Change in society's social values can follow.

The subject of such a book could be:

- o   a new paradigm

- o   a new philosophy

- o   a new arm of science

Those are only a few examples of the products of wisdom.

Emotional States

This character will have little negativity because he consciously spends time filtering it out whenever it rises into their mind and will gain a pure joy and peace from their wisdom and humility.

Chain of Events for this Character

In the case of the given character above, the chain of events in the way they see things is as follows:

- o   They are connected to the truths of their inner-self and can see the true meaning to life

- o   Contemplation

- o   A continuous flow of insights and understanding from within themselves

- o   Recording their visions

- o   A simple pleasure derived

Assigning a Low Level of Awareness

Have a look at the following image:

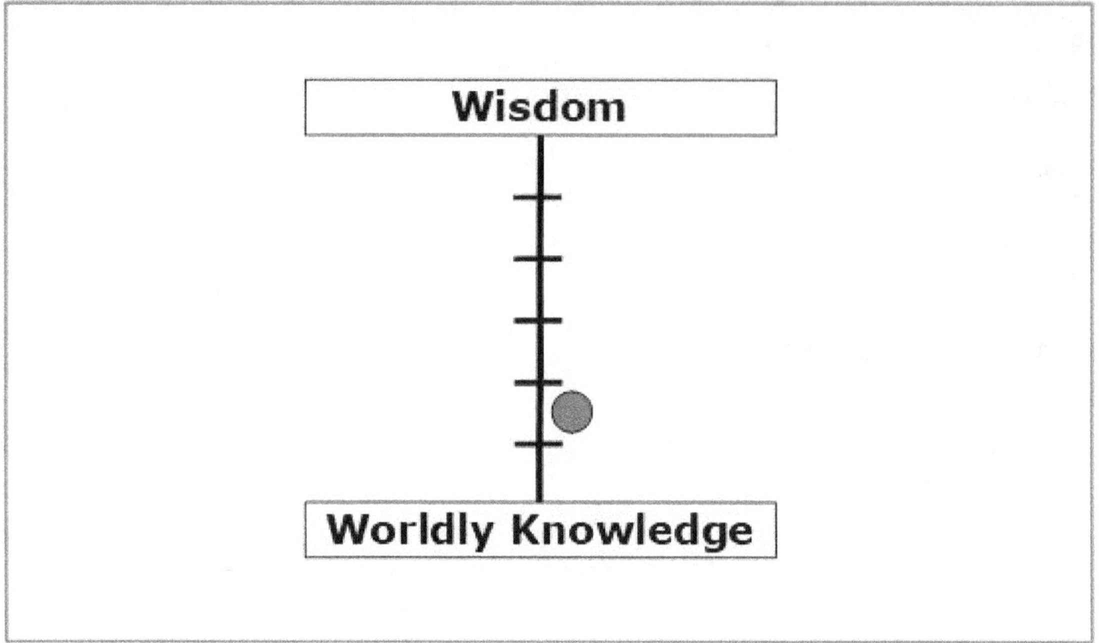

Awareness Level Scale: img 13

If instead, you assign a low level of awareness in wisdom for a character, then that character will be solely focused on their limited outer-self perspective.

The low awareness level in wisdom means that you have limited the character to the relevant knowledge and understanding as held by their mainstream society and to the errors inherent within that knowledge and understanding.

This low level of awareness in wisdom is what you will give to most characters because you need them to be full of errors. It also allows for plenty of room in which growth in awareness can take place throughout your storyline.

Motivations and Values

A character with this limited mainstream knowledge and understanding will have the following motivations and values:

- They will choose values that are presently in vogue in their society

- Will tend to imitate what others are doing without question, just to fit in

- Will develop lots of unnecessary wants, needs, and desires

- Will probably be indulgent and not very disciplined

- Will automatically accept things as they are without question

- Will have little intuition or insight into alternatives, and if they do,, they will dismiss them

- They know nothing about their true inner-self and so they will believe themselves to be their assumed outer-self-identity and will be subjected to the limitations and errors this belief imposes on them

- They will be more selfish than they are giving and sharing

- Their worldly social knowledge will be full of erroneous meaning.

- When things go wrong for them, they will point the finger of blame at others and society

Those are only a few examples of the lack of wisdom and error within a character. The list can go on forever.

This type of character can represent many themes because there is an infinite number of outer-self values and errors that you can assign to them during their creation stage.

You can create a hundred characters with the same low level of awareness for wisdom, and then be able to relate each to different combinations of motivations and values. In turn, this leads to entirely different behaviour from each of the one hundred characters, and all from the one given low awareness level for wisdom.

Imagine how many different characters you can create when you consider that there are ten truths to combine, each with several awareness levels. There is also an infinite number of outer-self values and behaviours you can assign to a character.

Emotional States

When a character with little wisdom has their wants, needs, and desires fulfilled, they will momentarily feel happy and will have some positive emotions to last them for a while.

But if something thwarts the fulfilment of their wants, needs, and desires, they can suddenly become full of anger and rage and other negative emotions.

You can google 'positive/negative emotions lists' to help you during your character creation stage. All you need to do is to select four or five positive and negative emotions from those lists for each character, and this is the way he or she will react and respond to other characters and events within your storyline.

But remember to let the theme a character will be representing to aid you in those emotional selections. For example, if 'Murder' is one of your issues, then you will need to select negative emotions such as anger, jealousy, or blind rage for the character who is likely to be the killer.

Chain of Events for this Character

In the case of the given character above, the chain of events in the way they see things is as follows:

- They have lost contact with the truths of their inner-self and can see no real meaning to life

- Their limited focus solely on their outer self brings them into error

- They prefer to accept things as they are rather than dispute them, just to fit in

- A large amount of their behaviour is an imitation

- They will develop lots of unnecessary wants, needs, and desires accompanied by swings in emotion and moods

- They blame others on their bad behaviour and their misfortunes

- They believe their true identity to be the extremely limited outer-self

Adding Other Truths and Their Antonyms

Remember, this chapter only covered one truth and its antonym along with selected awareness levels for a character. When you add a second truth and a third, along with an awareness level in them, it changes a character's motivations, choice of values, emotions, and actions.

For instance, in the last scale shown above for wisdom, if you also add the character's truth and antonym for 'Morality' and give them a low awareness level for this as well, then they will be involved with crime and the darker sides of life to fulfil their selfish needs.

You could then add a third truth, such as 'Creativity' and give them a high awareness level for this. Combining these three truths and their awareness levels would mean that the character is selfish, is immoral in how they fulfil their needs and will be creative in ways that are beneficial to themselves, but extremely harmful to others.

The more truths and antonyms and their awareness levels you add to a character, the more differences you can bring to the character's motivations, values, outlook, and actions. It is only a matter of working them out based on the theme a character will be representing.

CHAPTER 7

TRUTHS AND OUTER-SELF VALUES

'LOVE'

'Mind is not a dustbin to keep anger, hatred and jealousy. But is the treasure box to keep love, happiness, and sweet memories.'

Buddha

Courtesy of: e-buddha.com

Our fourth truth is 'Love.'

Assigning a High Level of Awareness

Have a look at the following image:

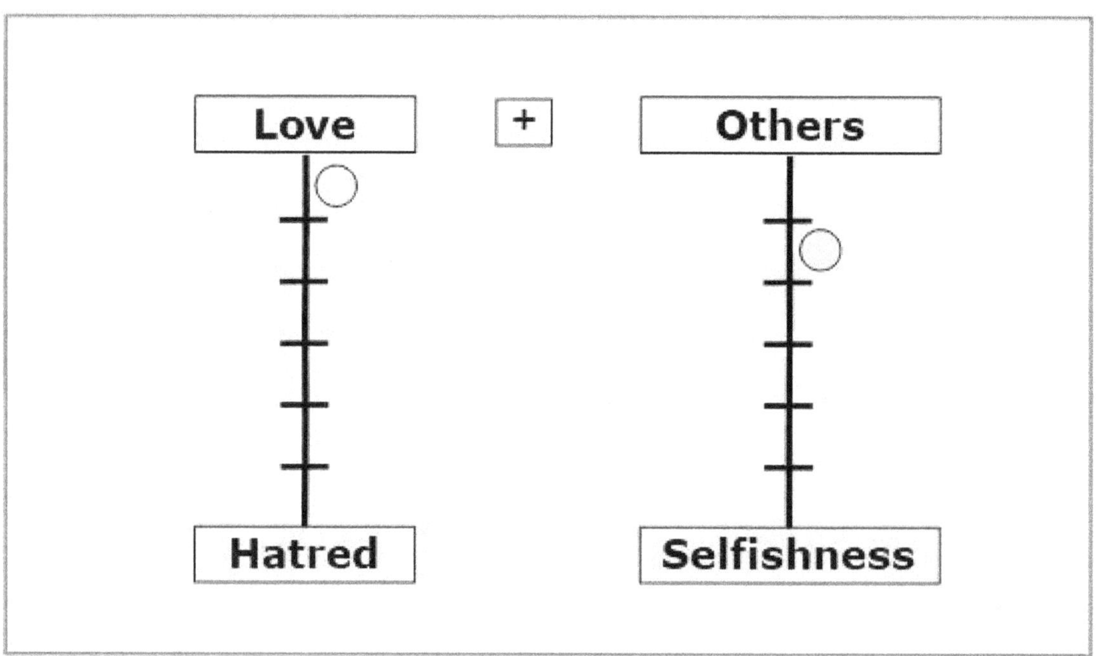

Awareness Level Scale: img 14

During the character creation stage, if you choose to give a character a high awareness level in love, you will also be providing them with a high awareness level in their treatment of 'Others.'

Motivations

This character will have the following motivations:

- They will deeply value their family members
- Respect their close friends
- Have unfailing loyalty
- Have benevolence and empathy for other characters
- Have kindness for animals
- Have a passion for life itself

Those are only a few examples of a character's deep sense of love and respect. You can assign these motivations to them during their creation stage.

Values

This character's deep inner sense of love will see him choosing the following values:

- They will find ways to show their love rather than say it
- Will be full of acts of kindness, gifts, and service
- Will listen and validate others
- Will make time for others
- Will be full of support and compliments for others
- They will celebrate the uniqueness of others

Those are just some of the values a character may have when they have this deep sense of true love.

If one of your themes in your book is 'Love versus Hatred' or 'Love versus Indifference' then these are the type of values, you will assign to your character who will represent the love side of the theme.

Emotional States

This character will be full of feelings of admiration, reverence, adoration, fondness, benevolence, affection, sympathy, enthusiasm, enchantment, yearning, romance and so on, and you can assign these sorts of feelings to a character who is full of love.

Chain of Events for this Character

In the case of the given character above, the chain of events in the way they see things is as follows:

- They are connected to the truths of their inner-self and can see the true meaning to life

- Will treasure and love their family and will be loyal to their friends

- Will be benevolent to others, and kind to animals

- Will have a passion for life

- Will choose values that enhance life for themselves and others

- They will continually experience positive emotions

Assigning a Low Level of Awareness

Have a look at the following image:

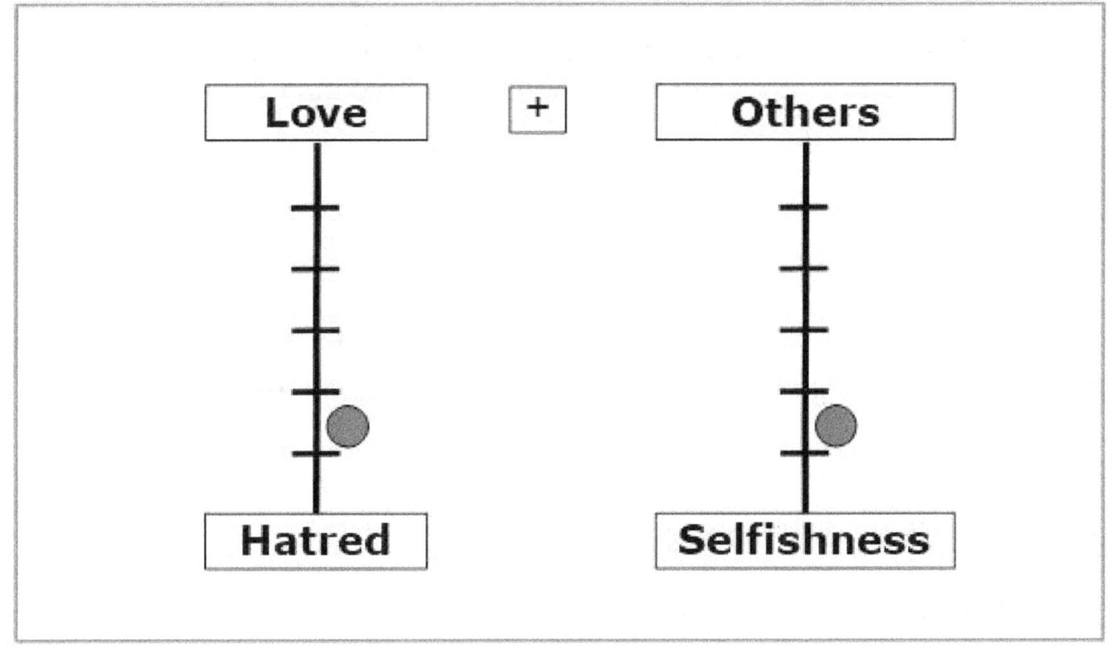

Awareness Level Scale: img 15

If instead, you assign a low awareness level for both 'Love' and 'Others' to a character, they will be selfish and will tend to hate others or be indifferent to them.

Motivations

This character will have the following negative motivations:

- They will be indifferent to the needs of those around them

- Will be full of animosity and hatred

- Will bear grudges and will be full of bitterness

- Will be full of disgust, aversion, and loathing

- Will be spiteful and insulting

- Will be full of malice and provocation

- They will be unfaithful and disrespectful

Remember, those are just some examples of hatred and indifference.

When creating a character for a theme such as 'Love versus Hatred' or 'Love versus Indifference,' you can assign those types of negative motivations to them during the character creation stage.

Values

A character with these hatreds and negativities will consider the following as values:

- o Deliberately causing divisions between people

- o Will be dishonest and blaming others on the way they are

- o Has unreasonable adverse reactions to other opinions

- o Deliberately plays into the anxiety and fears of others

- o Their cynical attitude generates resentment and jealousy

- o Attempting to hurt others

Emotional States

This character will be full of unfriendliness, dislike, hostility, antagonism, hate, ill-will, spite, aversion, prejudice, and racialism. You can find lists of negative emotions online or within a thesaurus.

Chain of Events for this Character

In the case of the given character above, the chain of events in the way they see things is as follows:

- o They have lost contact with the truths of their inner-self and can see no real meaning to life

- o They will be indifferent to others or will project their negativity onto them

- o   Will point the finger of blame at their society and others

- o   They will be continually cynical about everything

CHAPTER 8

TRUTHS AND OUTER-SELF VALUES

'MORALITY'

'Conventionality is not morality.'

Charlotte Bronte

Courtesy of: Daily Quotes

Our fifth truth is 'Morality,' and in this book, it refers to how a character lives at both their individual and social levels.

Have a look at the following image:

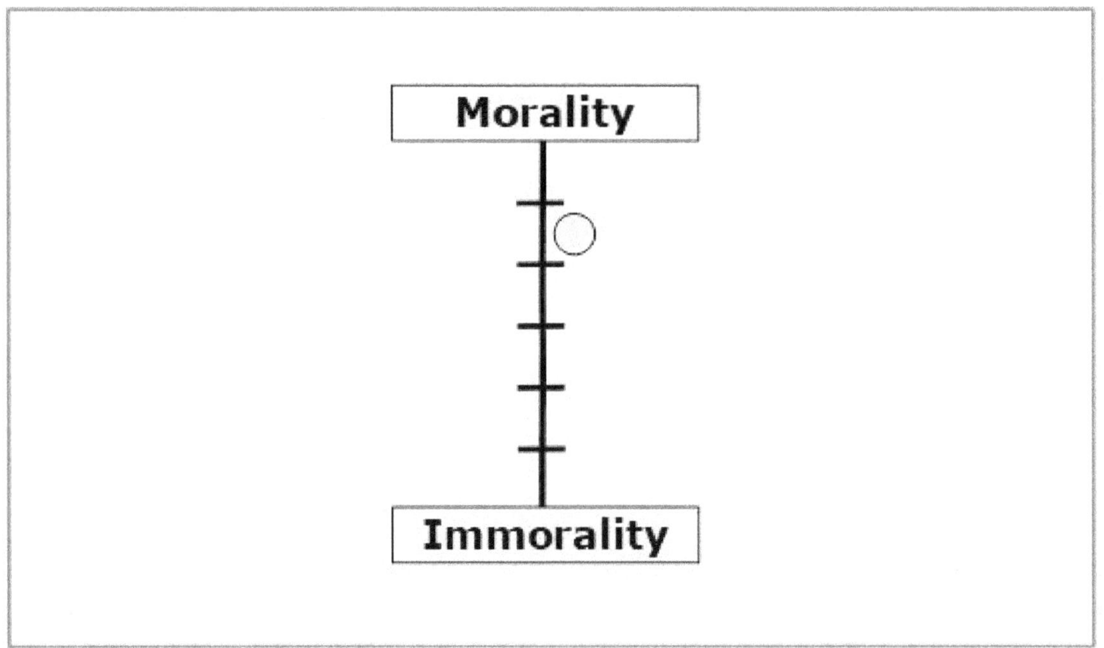

Awareness Level Scale: img 16

Assigning a High Level of Awareness

During the character creation stage, if you choose to give them a high awareness level for their 'Morality', you can give them some higher awareness levels with some of their other truths as well.

Motivations

A character with a high moral sense guiding them in their decisions and actions will be motivated in the following way:

- They will be aware of their motivations and how their choices and their actions will affect others
- Will be very responsible for their social duties and obligations
- Will have integrity and will be lawful
- Will be just and fair to everyone
- Will have lots of moral courage and moral strength
- Will have inner resistance to being corrupted
- Will be commendable and praiseworthy
- They will have their heart in the right place

Those are only a few examples of a character's motivations if they possess an elevated moral sense.

Values

This character's high moral sense will attract them to the following outer-self values:

- To set good examples and be a good role model for others
- Will fight for justice
- Will value their duties, their obligations, and their conduct
- They will value wisdom, knowledge, temperance, empathy, and fairness

If one of your themes in your book is 'Morality versus Vice', then these are the type of qualities and values you will assign to a character representing the Morality side of the theme.

Emotional States

This character's honesty and integrity will bring with it a continuous release of positive emotions.

Chain of Events for this Character

In the case of the given character above, the chain of events in the way they see things is as follows:

- o They are connected to the truths of their inner-self and can see the true meaning to life

- o They will be continually aware of their motivations

- o Will be highly responsible and fair to others

- o Will be resistant to corruption

- o They will let their sense of duty and their heart guide them

Assigning a Low Level of Awareness

Have a look at the following image:

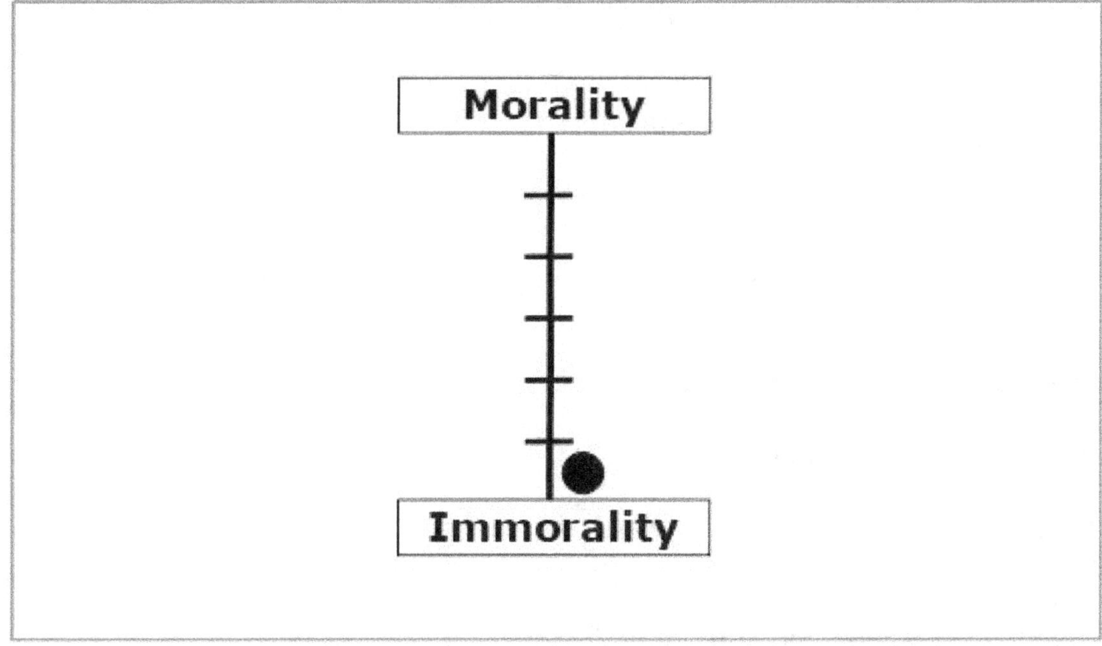

Awareness Level Scale: img 17

If instead, you choose to give a low awareness level for their sense of 'Morality,' the character will lack those higher moral qualities as listed with the character above.

By assigning a low level of awareness in Morality for a character, you are effectively depriving them of moral guidance in their reasoning, in their choices, and their actions. During your storyline, their immorality should plummet to even deeper levels than you initially assigned to them.

Motivations

With no moral sense guiding a character:

- They will be morally degenerate
- Will feel no shame or embarrassment for their actions
- Will feel no remorse for what they have done to others
- Will always attempt to rationalise and explain away what they have done
- Gets involved in immoral activity but insists to themselves and others that they are moral

- Tends to be irresponsible

- Has little resistance or filters on their behaviour

- Will be dishonest and inconsiderate of others

- Will be highly likely to break their society's moral code and to break the law.

- Will have unethical behaviour towards others

- Will not see the harm they do to others

- Will be focused solely on what they want and does not see their motivations and intent

- They will eventually descend into immoral oblivion

Remember, those are just some examples of a character's motivation without the light of Morality guiding them.

Values

A character with those immoral motivations listed above will be attracted to what they consider as values:

- They will be involved in fraud and deception for their benefit

- Will quickly become involved with crime

- Will take the law into their own hands to solve their disputes, usually in a violent way

- Will be involved in murder, serial killing, and psychopathic behaviour

- In the worse possible cases, they can be responsible for such things as serial murders, mass atrocities, slavery, or genocide

- They will abandon the little moral sense they might have in pursuit of their social ambitions

o   Their immoral behaviour will bring them into contact with other corrupt characters, into contact with the law, and into the courts as society demands justice for their crimes

That list above contains only a few examples of immoral behaviour.

This character can represent the 'Vice' side of your theme. You can assign those types of immoral behaviours and values to them during the character creation stage.

All novels and plays need highly flawed characters, and just by assigning a low level of awareness in 'Morality,' you can have as many of these characters as you need.

Emotional States

Because of this character's behaviour, ranging from dishonesty to murder, they will be full of negative emotions such as resentment, jealousy, avarice, greed, anger, hostility, hatred, rage and so on.

Chain of Events for this Character

In the case of the given character above, the chain of events in the way they see things is as follows:

o   They have lost contact with the truths of their inner-self and can see no real meaning to life

o   Without a moral sense guiding them, they have no filters on their choices and actions

o   Will break every law to get what they want

o   Will be involved with like-minded characters

o   The justice system eventually catches up with them

CHAPTER 9

TRUTHS AND OUTER-SELF VALUES

'OTHERS'

'Peace can only come as a natural consequence of universal enlightenment and merging of races, and we are still far from this blissful realisation.'

Nicola Tesla

Courtesy of: www.goalcast.com

Our sixth truth is 'Others.' 'Others' in this book refers to how a character sees other characters and how they choose to treat them.

Have a look at the following image:

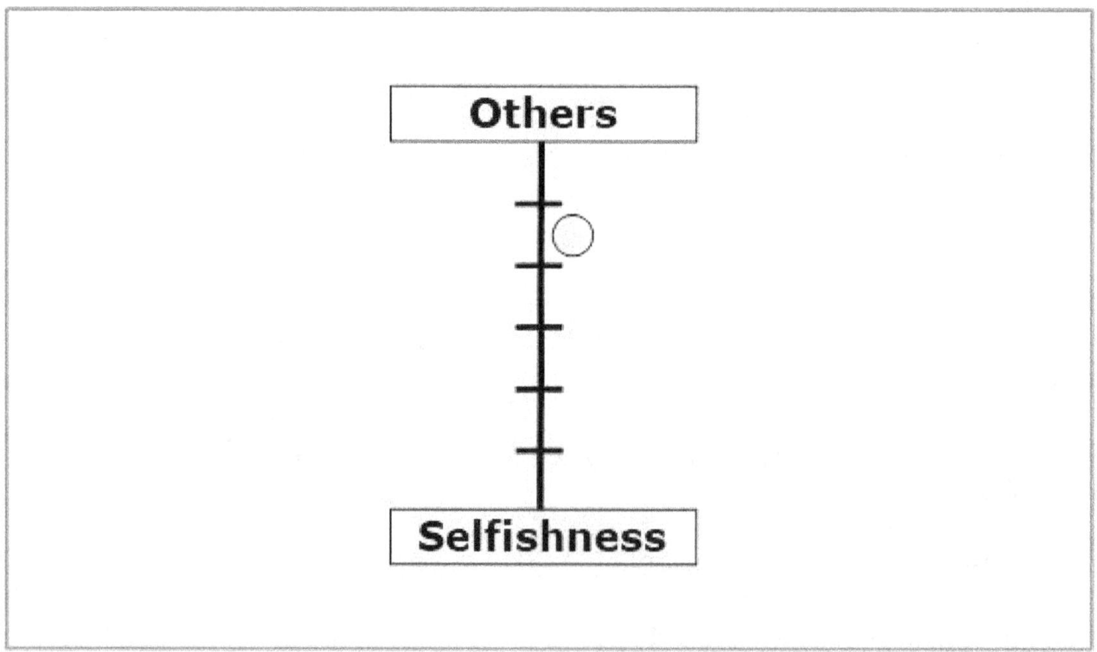

Awareness Level Scale: img 18

Assigning a High Level of Awareness

During the character creation stage, if you choose to give them a high level of awareness for 'Others', you can also give them a high level of appreciation for some of their other truths, especially in morality. You will then have a character who is highly motivated to be in the service of helping others and doing good things.

Motivations

A character with a deep concern for 'Others' guiding them in their decisions and actions will have the following motivations:

- Selflessness, compassion, empathy, generosity, giving, kindness, humility, forgiveness, and respect

- They will have a deep concern for the welfare and happiness of others

- Will have a robust heartfelt desire to help those people who are suffering and will want to see all suffering coming to an end

- Will see all people as equal and will help anyone who needs it

- They do not need their charitable deeds to be known

- They will not expect a return for the help they gives

- They are prepared to make sacrifices for others

- If pushed, they are capable of heroic deeds

Those are only a few examples of the motivations a character will have if they have a high level of awareness and concern for others.

If one of your themes in your book is 'Others versus Selfishness' then these are the types of motivations you will assign to a character representing the 'Others' side of the theme.

Values

This character's deeply felt need to help others will attract them to the following outer-self values:

- Fairness, charity, community, compassion, prosperity, and equality

- Volunteering to help during national disasters

- They will not necessarily be interested in owning possessions

- Will have concern for people and animals

- Will make every effort to bring change for the better for all

- Will be seeking a higher quality of life for the less fortunate in society

- Will have an urgent concern for the poor, the helpless and defenceless, the oppressed, and will want to do something about it

- They will be prepared to help others even at a cost to themselves

- If they possess social wealth, then others will benefit

Again, this is only a small list of possible values the character will have.

Emotional States

A character with this need to help others while taking the necessary action will be experiencing positive emotions and fulfilment in life.

Chain of Events for this Character

In the case of the given character above, the chain of events in the way they see things is as follows:

- They are connected to the truths of their inner-self and can see the true meaning to life

- They are highly motivated to seek ways to help others

- They always put others first

- They will be involved in institutions and charities that help the sick and the poor

- They seek to improve society in many ways

Assigning a Low Level of Awareness

Have a look at the following image:

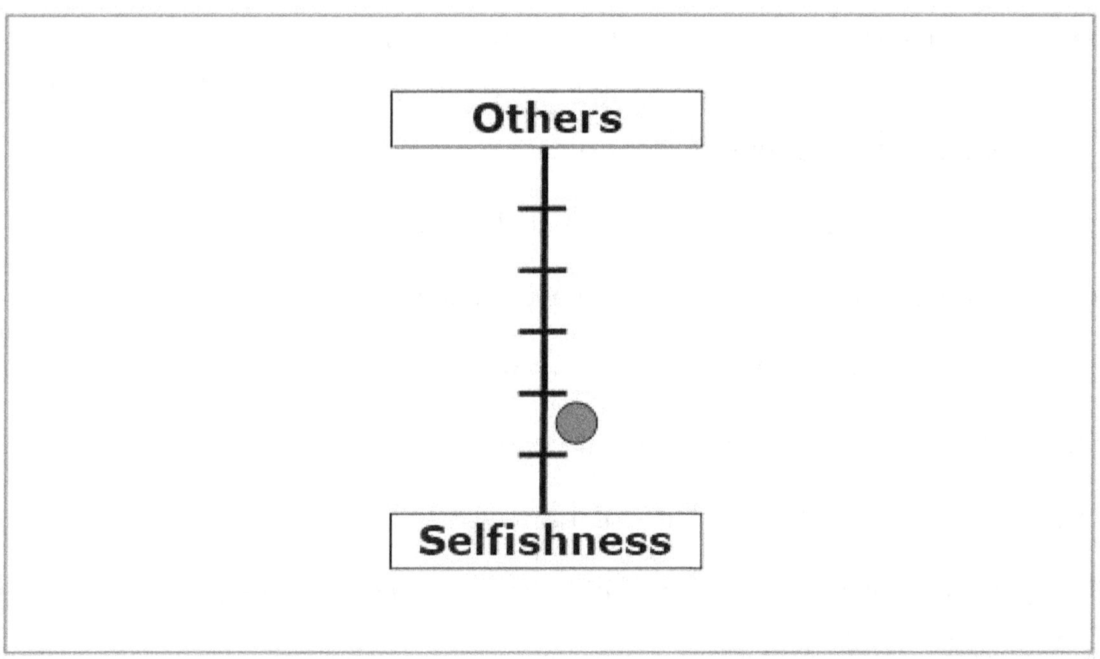

Awareness Level Scale: img 19

If instead, you choose to give a character a low awareness level in concern for 'Others' they will be selfish by nature. They will lack the higher qualities as listed with the character above. They will be solely focused on what they can get for themselves..

Motivations

With no concern for others guiding a character's choices and their actions, the character will have the following motivations:

- They only understand their identity in terms of their individuality and have no awareness of their collective nature. They cannot have a deep understanding of others.

- They will be self-centred and likely to be narcissistic

- Will not have any regard for others in the pursuit of their welfare and fulfilling their own needs

- Will only have a concern for what they can get for themselves even to the extent of hurting others in the process

- Will be mean and ungenerous

- Will not be very cooperative with others and will not be a good team player

- Will have little compassion and tolerance for others

- Will not be supportive of others and will be unlikely to share

- Will not be thoughtful of others and not be very welcoming

- If they are narcissistic, they might be full of pretensions and airs

- They will tend to project blame for what they do onto others

- Will have a bloated and unrealistic opinion of themselves

- Will see themselves as being at the centre of their world with everyone else gravitating around them

- Will have a love of how they imagine and visualise themselves and responds to that

- They will be arrogant and boastful

- Their favourite words are 'I' 'Me' 'Myself'

Those are only a few examples of the motivations a character can have if they have a low awareness level in their concern for others.

In a book theme such as 'Others versus Selfishness' then these are the types of motivations you will assign to a character representing the 'Selfishness' side of the issue.

Values

This selfish character will have the following values:

- They will seek things that serve their fulfilment

- Anything on the economic list that will enhance their benefit, pleasure, and welfare

In the very act of being selfish, this character will deprive themselves of growing in love and empathy for others. They will also be denying themselves the opportunity to use their free-will in choosing higher values and so they shut themselves out of the growth in wisdom and in fulfilling their inner-self purpose to evolve.

Emotional States

This character's selfish choices and acts negatively play into their emotional level. It depresses their need to grow in concern for others, and this releases the whole spectrum of negative emotions to their outer-self-conscious awareness. For instance, they will be angry at anything and everyone who gets in the way of them getting what they need, want, and desire. They will project negative emotions, such as hatred and rage.

Chain of Events for this Character

In the case of the given character above, the chain of events in the way they see things is as follows:

- They have lost contact with the truths of their inner-self and can see no real meaning to life

- They are mainly focused on themselves and sees themselves as the centre of the universe

- Will put themselves first and shows no real concern for others

- Will project their negative feelings onto others

- Will blame society and others for their miseries

- They live in words such as 'I' 'Me' 'Myself'

CHAPTER 10

TRUTHS AND OUTER-SELF VALUES

'CREATIVITY'

'Thank goodness I was never sent to school; it would have rubbed off some of the originality.'

Beatrix Potter

Courtesy of: Daily Quotes

Our seventh truth is 'Creativity.' Creativity is the ability to come up with new things. A character can use this ability for the good of themselves and others, or they might use it in a way that can bring misery and destruction.

Have a look at the following image:

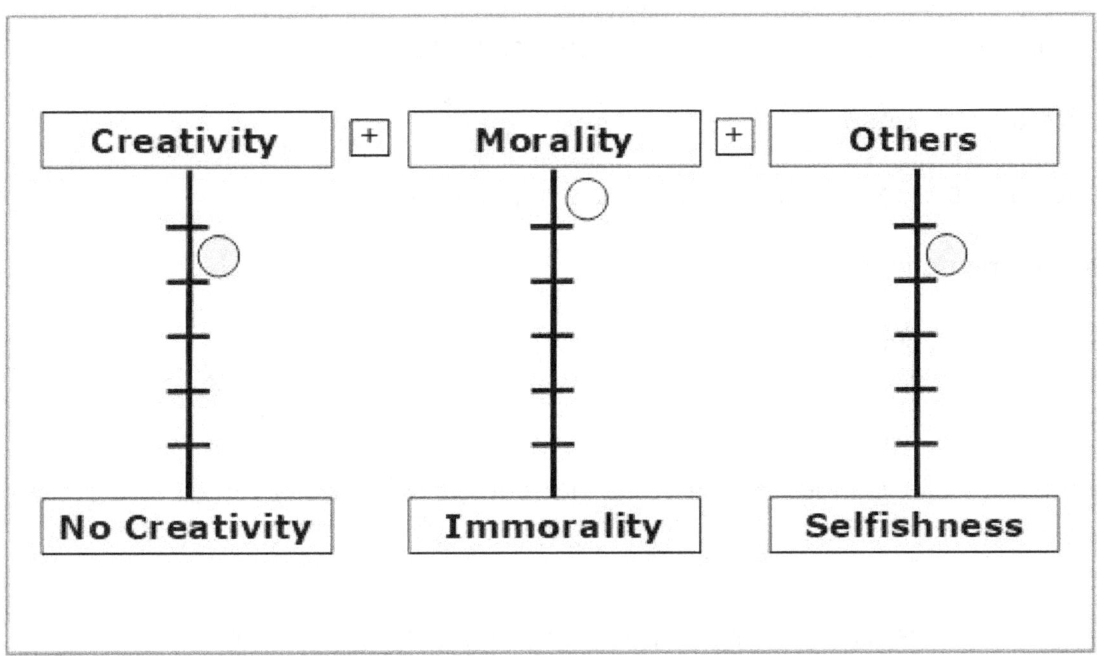

Awareness Level Scale: img 20

Assigning a High Level of Awareness

As you can see, I have combined three of the truths in the image above and have given all three a high awareness level. As I said before, each truth and its awareness level influence every other truth before being projected out to affect the conscious mind and behaviour of a character.

A character with high awareness levels in those truths above will be highly creative with a deep sense of morality guiding their creations. At the same time, they will create things that are valuable and beneficial for others and for the progress of their society.

Motivations

This character will have the following inner motivations:

- o Feels the need to find self-expression in creative works
- o Does not conform to mainstream fixed beliefs and attitudes
- o Thinks outside of the box and has alternative ideas
- o Has inner vision and generates unique and beneficial ideas
- o Has an active critical sense
- o Perseverance in the face of initial rejection and opposition
- o Creates new combinations of ideas
- o Has a deep aesthetic sense

Those are only a few examples of the inner motivations that can go with the given truths above.

If one of your themes in your book is 'Good versus Bad' then these are the types of motives you can assign to a character who will represent the 'Good' side of the theme.

Values

This character's high level of creativity and inner motivations will attract them to the following outer-self values:

- o   They will be open to new experiences

- o   Will be aware of problems they can solve with their creative efforts

- o   Will hold the positive creativity of others in high regard

- o   Will improve on what already exists

- o   Brain-storming and problem-solving

- o   Shows brilliance in what they create

- o   Their creations bring progress to society

- o   They will be an inspiration to others

That list above contains only a few values a character with high awareness levels for 'Creativeness,' 'Morality,' and 'Others' might have.

Emotional States

Self-actualisation through creativity brings fulfilment and happiness to the character. This fulfilment and happiness are enhanced when creativity is moral, and it improves society and enhances the lives of others. The character's passion for creativity leads to lots of enjoyment and positive feelings.

Chain of Events for this Character

In the case of the given character above, the chain of events in the way they see things is as follows:

- o   They are connected to the truths of their inner-self and can see the true meaning to life

- o   They experience their inner creative urge

- o They also feel the need to be creative in beneficial ways for the good of others

- o They will feel the need to be original and unique

- o They resist opposition to their creations because they can see the great potential in them

- o They respect other creative people and their creations

Assigning a Low Level of Awareness

Have a look at the following image:

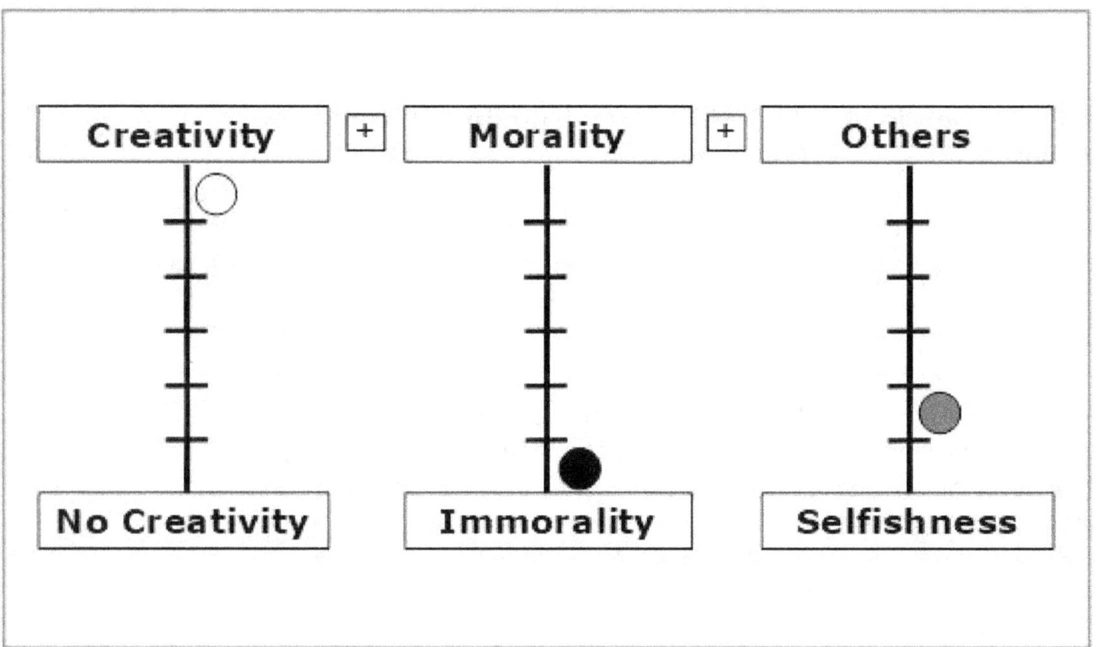

Awareness Level Scale: img 21

Again, in the image above, I have combined the same three truths. In this example, the character's creativity remains high, but has been given low awareness levels for both 'Morality' and 'Others.'

The above combined low awareness levels within a character will see them involved with the dark side of creativity.

If you give a character those specific awareness levels in those truths, they will have inner motivations that can pose a severe threat to the well-being of others and their society.

This type of character can play the role of many themes, such as 'Good versus Bad.'

Motivations

With those assigned awareness levels, you can give the character the following motivations:

- In everyday life, they will betray, cheat, and lie
- They will be deceptive for their benefit
- They will be manipulative of others for their gain
- They will tend to outwit others
- They will have criminal intent
- They will be dangerous and intimidating
- They will have malevolent intent with their creativity
- They can become a psychopathic serial killer
- On a worldwide scale, they might use their creative abilities for terrorist purposes or something like a twisted political ideology

Those are only a few examples of the motivations a character can have with those awareness levels in the truths of Creativity, Morality, and Others.

Values

This character will see any of the following as values:

- o   Racism

- o   Weapons of destruction

- o   Twisted scientific experiments

- o   Deliberately harmful conspiracy theories

It should not be too difficult for you to add many more negative values to that list above.

Emotional States

They will be aggressive in what they want to achieve. They will not necessarily have emotions about what they do. But they will have malicious intent and a depraved satisfaction about the destruction and suffering they bring onto others and society. They will also have feelings of inadequacy, and their outer-self acts make them feel powerful.

Chain of Events for this Character

In the case of the given character above, the chain of events in the way they see things is as follows:

- o   They have lost contact with the truths of their inner-self and can see no real meaning to life

- o   They will be malevolent in their intent with whatever they create

- o   Will be deceptive and manipulative

- o   Will more than likely progress to more significant crimes

- o   They will pose a growing threat to their wider society

CHAPTER 11

TRUTHS AND OUTER-SELF VALUES

'ALL-POSSIBILITY'

'Others have seen what is and asked why.
I have seen what could be and asked why not.'

Pablo Picasso

Courtesy of: Daily Quotes

Our eighth inner-self truth is 'All-Possibility.' We will have a look at how the character's awareness level of this truth affects them on their outer-self behaviour.

Assigning a High Level of Awareness

Have a look at the following image:

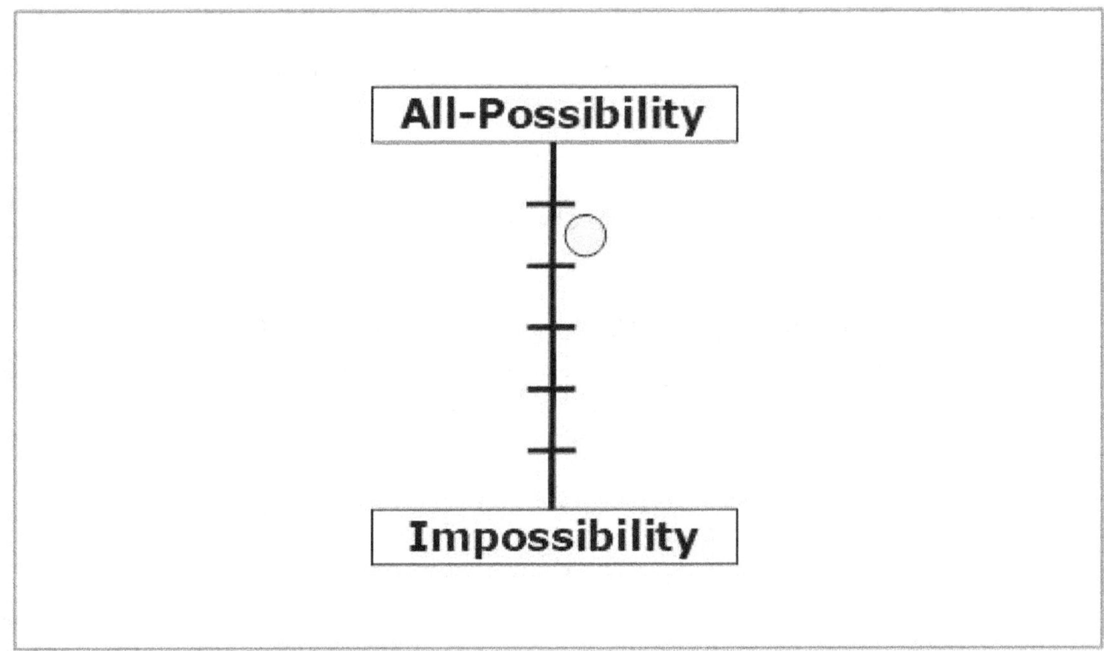

Awareness Level Scale: img 22

In the image above I have given a high awareness level for 'All-Possibility.' 'All-Possibility' is the awareness that we can continuously become more than we are at any given time if we have the intent and if we make the efforts.

Motivations

A character with a high awareness level in 'All-Possibility' will have the following inner-self motivations:

- o   They will be full of optimism and will find more joy in life

- o   Their positive outlook will generate well-being within them

- o   They factor in all-possibility into their interpretations

- o   Their happiness is found within them rather than outside of them

- o   They always look to achieve the best possible results

- o   They are rarely pessimistic

- o   They know that they aren't limited to just what they can see in front of them

- o   Their sense of the all-possible allows them to glimpse their immortality

Those are only a few examples of the inner motivations this character will have.

If one of your themes in your book is 'Positive versus Negative' then these are the types of inner motives you can assign to the character representing the Positive side of the theme.

Values

This character's enhanced sense of 'All-Possibility' will lead them towards the following outer-self values:

- o   They believe that progress is always possible with anything

- o   They see the intrinsic value and meaning of life

- o   Their positive outlook enhances their values such as their relationships, happiness, and life-satisfaction

- o   Their values will be goals that continuously improve them on their inner-self

- o   Their choice of values is always compatible with their inner-self purpose to evolve

- o   Over time, their choice of values will bring them more wisdom, and a more profound sense of love and empathy for others

- o   Their choice of values will lead them to the continual experience of positive emotions

- o   They see potential everywhere rather than just by comparison

- o   They also see all-possibility for others

Those are only a few of the values a character possessing an elevated awareness in 'All-Possibility' might have.

Emotional States

This character will experience the whole spectrum of positive feelings and so will have lots of joy in life. Their positive emotions spring from their sense that anything is possible.

Chain of Events for this Character

In the case of the given character above, the chain of events in the way they see things is as follows:

- o   They are connected to the truths of their inner-self and can see the true meaning to life

- o They will experience an inner-self sense of all-possibility

- o This sense of all-possibility forms the basis of their interpretations of experience

- o This sense of all-possibility generates a positive outlook in life from both an emotional and a mental perspective

- o They realise that happiness begins within them rather than without

- o They seek continual improvement for themselves and others

Assigning a Low Level of Awareness

Have a look at the following image:

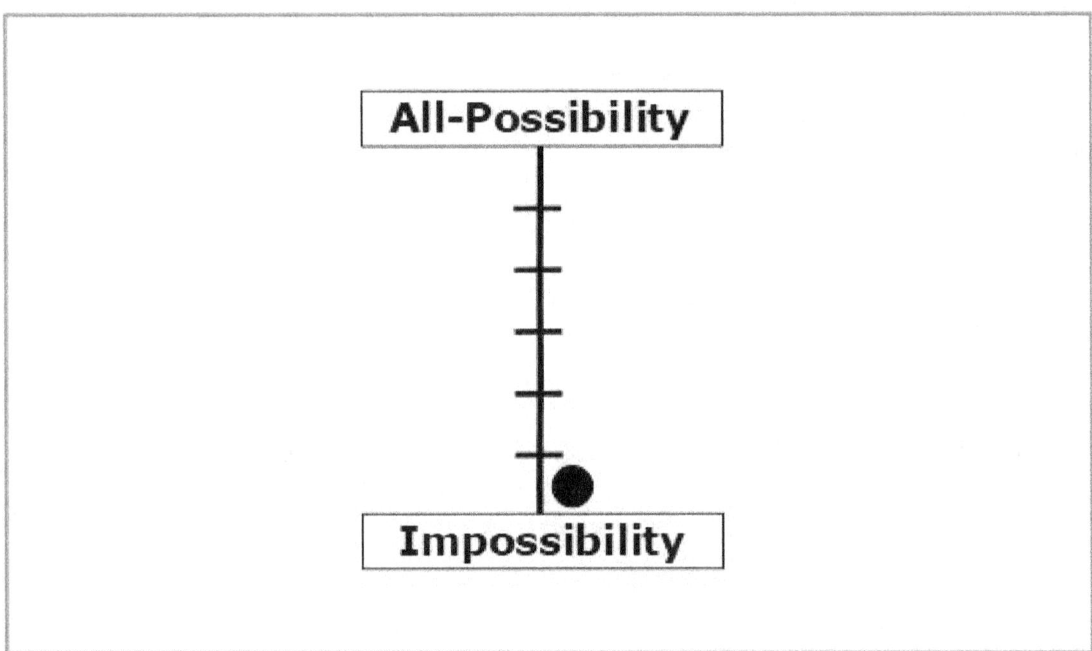

Awareness Level Scale: img 23

In the image above, I have given the character the lowest level of awareness for 'All-Possibility.' A character having this sense of the impossible operating within their interpretations will have some of the following negative motivations:

Motivations

They see impossibility; hopelessness; no choice whatsoever; cannot conceive positive alternatives; always thinks of things as unattainable; obstacles are insurmountable; everywhere as inaccessible.

- o They believe things are set in stone and cannot be changed

- o They visualise the worst possible situations and outcomes

- o They see boundaries, confinement, and limitations everywhere

- o They always feel that they have no control over their life

- o They have dysfunctional and self-defeating behaviour

- o They hang onto destructive relationships

- o Fear of failure stops them from achieving anything. Their constant fear about it not being perfect makes them pessimistic

- o Their pessimism colours their interpretations and understanding of events and others

- o They imagine themselves to be extremely limited and restrictive even though this is not the true situation with their all-possibility inner-self.

- o They suffer from tiredness and little stamina

Those are only a few examples of the motivations a character can have if they are given a low awareness level in the truth of 'All-Possibility.'

Values

This character will irrationally hold some of the following as values:

- o Always trying for unattainable and unrealistic goals, and when they fail, they become extremely pessimistic. They cannot accept failures and becomes overwhelmed rather than learning from them

- o They see the hopes, dreams, and expectations of an optimist as irrational and impossible

- They believe that everything is senseless and absurd, including their existence

- Because they solely focus on their limited outer-self world, their happiness becomes dependent on the possession of external things

- They never embrace life as it is. If they do embrace what is in front of them, it is usually pleasure-based to make them feel good, rather than being improvement and growth-based.

- They do not believe progress is possible with anything

- The disconnection from the truths of their inner-self leads them to believe that life has no intrinsic meaning or value.

- The search for happiness solely in their outer-self world only heightens the sense of the impossible and deepens their unhappiness

- They see comparison everywhere rather than potential

- All their outer-self-satisfactions are temporary before their chronic state of pessimism and misery returns

Emotional States

- Unstable emotions

- Bad reactions to stress

- They take their errors and failures too seriously

- They suffer from boredom, anxiety, anger, guilt, shame, lack of confidence, and low emotional and mental well-being

- They suffer from depressive-like emotional states

Chain of Events for this Character

In the case of the given character above, the chain of events in the way they see things is as follows:

- o They have lost contact with the truths of their inner-self and can see no real meaning to life

- o They experience a sense of the impossible and becomes pessimistic

- o Their pessimism then plays into their imagination and their thoughts

- o They become emotionally negative about everything

The belief in the impossible about achieving anything will cause those negativities. Everything attempted is actively undermined by the character themselves. For example, they might be highly creative, but are reluctant to reveal this to others. A little voice within their head is telling them that they are not good enough and will not be accepted.

Remember to try out another truth or two with various levels of awareness given to them with the sense of all-possibility or impossibility. The permutations in outer-self behaviour appear to be infinite.

CHAPTER 12

TRUTHS AND OUTER-SELF VALUES

'IMMORTALITY'

'Life is the childhood of our immortality.'

Johann Wolfgang von Goethe

Courtesy of: MD Interactive

Our ninth inner-self truth is 'Immortality.' We will have a look at how the character's awareness level of this truth affects them on their outer-self side.

Assigning a High Level of Awareness

Have a look at the following image:

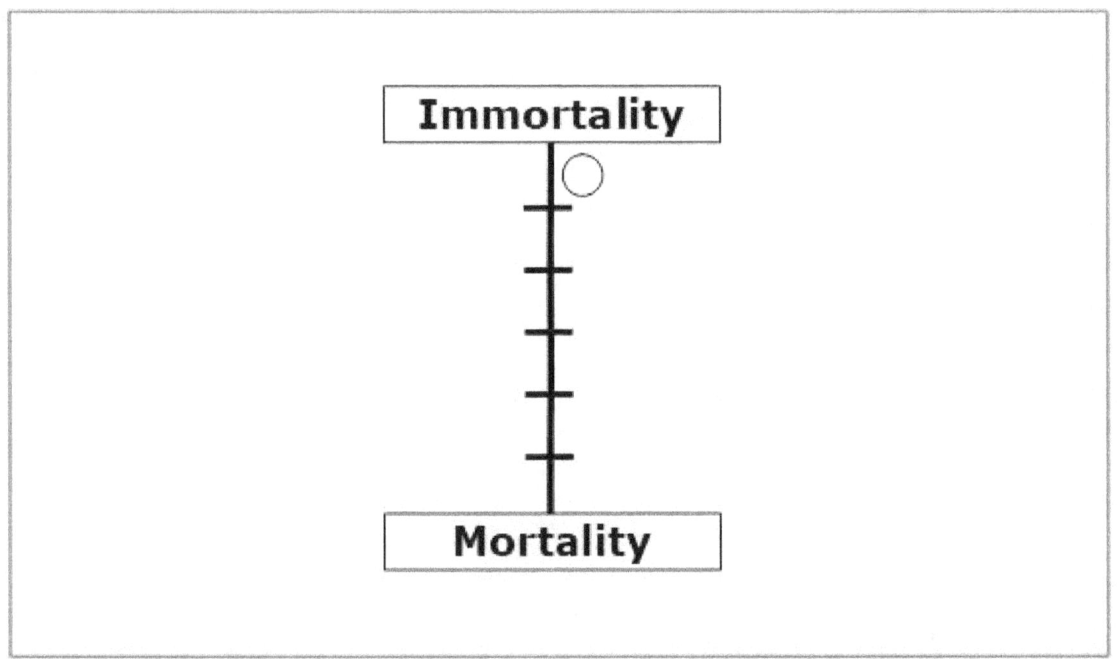

Awareness Level Scale: img 24

In the image above, I have given a high awareness level for 'Immortality.'

'Immortality' is an awareness that we live beyond physical death. Only certain characters will possess this high awareness level in their immortality.

Motivations

A character with a high awareness level in their 'Immortality' will have the following inner-self motivations:

- o They are connected to the truths of their inner-self and can see the true meaning to life

- o They intuitively know their physical death is not their end. They know their inner-self or consciousness will continue onwards

- o They have no underlying fear or terror of their outer-self physical death emerging into their interpretations and understanding

- o They will tend to be brave, have courage, and will be fearless in the face of adverse events

- o They never worry about what they have not achieved because they have no underlying fear of final death

Those are only a few examples of what motivates a character who has a sure inner-sense of their inner-self immortality.

A Deeper Look

But let us take a more in-depth look into what the awareness of being immortal means when it comes to this character's levels of awareness in their other truths. As I said in an earlier chapter, the awareness level in each truth not only affects a character's outer-self behaviour but also affects the character's awareness level of every other truth. So here are a few examples of how the awareness of inner-self immortality affects a character's awareness level in his other truths. Have a look at the following table containing all ten truths:

Immortality	A high awareness of their Inner-Self Immortality

Purpose to Evolve	They perceive their purpose to evolve through the awareness of their inner-self immortality
Free-Will	Their free-will is a dynamic flux with little limitations perceived
Wisdom	They grow in wisdom as they're not solely focused on outer-self worldly knowledge
Love	They experience deep inner-self-love and the whole spectrum of positive feelings that come with it
Morality	They will continually evolve in their morality
Others	They see beyond themselves and develops empathy and concern for others
Creativeness	Their positive outlook opens their creative abilities
All-Possibility	They see that everything can be changed and improved
Self-Identity	They realise their true inner-self-identity on both the individual and collective levels

This character will have high levels of awareness in all their inner-self truths that project out as their motivations, their values, and as their behaviour.

Values

This character's high awareness of their inner-self immortality will drive them towards the following outer-self values:

- o Cares less about themselves and more about others

- o Has little interest with things beyond the basics of life and seeks more fulfilling and longer lasting simple goals

- o They will hold a strong belief in the afterlife

That shortlist above contains only a few values a character with a high awareness level for 'Immortality' might have.

Emotional States

This character will have the following emotional outlook:

- o Their awareness of inner-self immortality enters their interpretations and understanding, and so they have no reasons to fear physical outer-self death or demise

- o This awareness of inner-self immortality increases their well-being, allows them better coping skills in life, and keeps them mentally and emotionally positive and healthy

- o They have little or no negative feelings that prevent them from achieving their goals in life

- o They see the real meaning to life because of the high awareness of their inner-self truths

Chain of Events for this Character

In the case of the given character above, the chain of events in the way they see things is as follows:

- o They are connected to the truths of their inner-self and can see the true meaning to life

- o They intuitively know they do not come to an end at their physical demise.

- o They realise a bigger purpose to life than just that presented to them by their outer-self world

- o They remain mentally and emotionally positive as they set about achieving goals with long-lasting meaning for themselves and others

Assigning a Low Level of Awareness

Have a look at the following image:

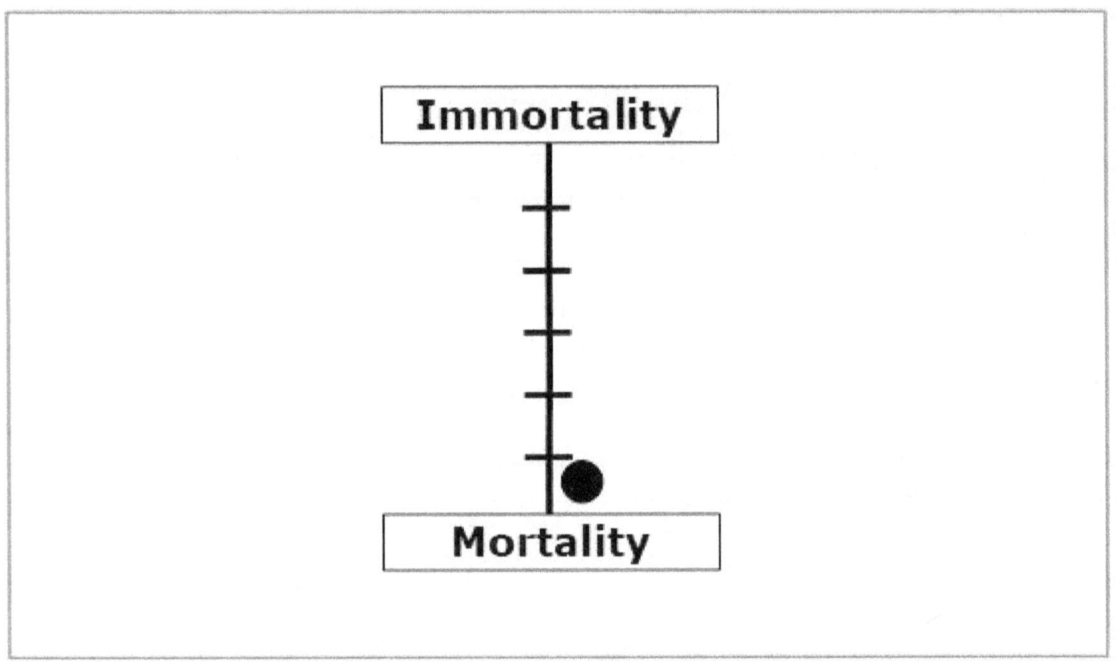

Awareness Level Scale: img 25

In the image above, I have given a low awareness level for 'Immortality.' If you assign a low awareness level for immortality to a character, it means they have no knowledge or understanding of the eternal nature of their inner self.

With the perception of being mortal and being subject to death, the character will have the following negative motivations:

Motivations

- o The perception that their physical outer-self will eventually come to an end generates fear in them.

- o This belief that their existence will end is at the root of all their thoughts, choices, and negative emotions

- o Demise, termination, extinction, death, end, last breath, last gasp, cease to be, end of one's days, to be all over, dead and gone are some of the words or language the character exists in

- o They have deep worries and extreme anxiety about what they have not achieved

- o Chances are, they have no religious or spiritual beliefs to comfort them

- o They will develop phobias related to the fear of death

Those are only a few examples of the motivations this character will have.

A Deeper Look

But let us take a more in-depth look into what the idea of being mortal or being subject to death means when it comes to this character's levels of awareness in their other truths. As I said in an earlier chapter, the awareness level of each truth not only affects a character's outer-self behaviour but also affects the character's awareness level of every other truth. So here are a few examples of how the idea of mortal death affects a character's awareness level in their other truths. Have a look at the following table containing the other nine truths:

Immortality	A low awareness of their Inner-Self Immortality
Purpose to Evolve	Without the awareness of their immortal inner-self, the character will also be completely unaware of their true purpose to evolve
Free-Will	Their free-will is frozen as they see limitations everywhere, including the ultimate restriction of death
Wisdom	They cannot grow in wisdom as they solely focus on outer-self worldly knowledge

Love	Instead of experiencing a deep inner-self-love, they suffer the whole spectrum of negative emotions, including fear, dread, anxiety, and hatred
Immorality	They are always vulnerable to descending into immorality
Others	They see themselves in a self-survival situation, them against others, and misses out on all opportunities to develop deep empathy and concern
Creativeness	Their cynical outlook puts a block on their innate creative abilities
All-Possibility	Rather than seeing all-possibility, they believe that everything is set-in-stone and cannot be changed, including themselves
Self-Identity	They never realise their true inner-self-identity neither on the individual level nor on the collective level

This character will have low levels of awareness in all their inner-self truths that project out as their motivations, their values, and as their behaviour.

Values

This character will have the following type of values:

- o Self-survival is their primary value

- o They spend their whole life chasing after things that have a temporary nature and do not last long. You find these things on the economic list

- o Power, Wealth, Fame for the wrong reasons

That list above contains only a few values a character with a low awareness level for 'Immortality' might have.

Emotional States

This character will experience the following emotions:

- o Without the awareness of the immortality of their inner-self influencing their interpretation and understanding, this character will experience fear and terror at the prospect of outer-self death and demise

- o The outer-self-belief that they will die and end abruptly, is incompatible with their true immortal inner-self nature

- o Their contemplation of death along with the fear and anxiety it generates reduces their well-being, reduces their coping skills in life, and gives them lots of emotional stress

- o This character's morbid fear of death prevents them from doing the things in life that they want to do. What is the point?

- o This character develops fears for the causes of death, such as disease or accidents. They will suffer from fear of being harmed and tends to see danger and risk everywhere

- o They suffer badly from sorrow, anxiety, pain, depression, and loneliness

- o Their narcissism and ego is intense

- o The reasons for this dark negative perception of life is that this character has no conscious connection to the truths of the inner-self and see no real meaning to their life

Chain of Events for this Character

In the case of the given character above, the chain of events in the way they see things is as follows:

- o They have lost contact with the truths of their inner-self and can see no real meaning to life

- o They experience the dread and fear of death and an end to who they think they are

- o They have no answers or no way of coping with that perception of death

- o Their mind and emotions become permeated with that fear of death, and in the process, they block out the truths of their inner self. They block out the true meaning to life.

- o They then go on to seek outer-self values that are also temporary in nature, matching their self-evaluation and the perception of themselves

Traditional Character Creation Elements

Following the creation of a character's inner-self using the alternative method presented in this book, you can then add on the traditional elements of character creation. These traditional elements are character history, descriptions through actions, anecdotes, dialogue, character differences, five sense descriptions of the character, focusing on detail, and describing mannerisms.

With the combination of both the alternative and traditional approach, you now have in place working psychology for the character as a reference point before you begin writing something.

(a) You have a complete understanding of your character to add to those traditional elements.

(b) You have both the inner-self and outer-self of a character.

(c) You have a multi-dimensional view of your character rather than just a flat 2-dimensional view.

In other words, you have an entire holistic understanding of your character. You are armed more than you've ever been to bring that character alive within your storyline, as well as entertaining and to delight your readers.

Character Physical Profile

Most writers find this area of character creation to be the most effortless and most natural part of the process. If you are finding this area as stressful, there are plenty of constructive tips online to help you with creating a character's physical appearance.

But while deciding on a character's physical appearance, you should also refer to the inner truths and their awareness levels you have already assigned to a character. For instance, in a traditional character build, a wise man might have long silver hair and beard. Or a criminal might have scars on their face.

Final Note

Before we move on to the tenth truth, the first nine truths I have covered so far are more than adequate in their scope to encompass an infinite number of motivations, values, and behaviour for all characters.

The tenth and final truth is 'Inner-Self Identity.' Inner-self-identity is an optional truth giving a more in-depth explanation as to the WHYs of a character's behaviour.

This tenth truth slightly brings you into the realm of spirituality or consciousness to show you a deeper meaning to what the outer-self and the inner-self of a character is. It shows you a deeper meaning to all the truths we have covered so far. I have already mentioned some of this deeper meaning earlier with the truths of 'All-Possibility' and 'Immortality.'

The tenth truth shows you more about the relationship between the Two Selves of a character to reveal more about their motivations, their values, and their behaviour.

But as I said already, the following tenth truth is optional, and you do not need to go any further unless you have intentions of adding spiritual or consciousness attributes to your characters.

CHAPTER 13

TRUTHS AND OUTER-SELF VALUES

'INNER-SELF IDENTITY'

' If an egg is broken by outside force, life ends.
If broken by inside force, life begins.
Great things always begin from inside.'

Buddha

Courtesy of: e-buddha.com

Our tenth truth is 'Inner-Self Identity.'

Simply put, the nine truths we have already covered, collectively make up the nature of a character's true inner-self-identity. When a character realises and evolves in those nine truths, the realisation of true inner-self-identity follows.

Inner-Self Identity

Have a look at the following image:

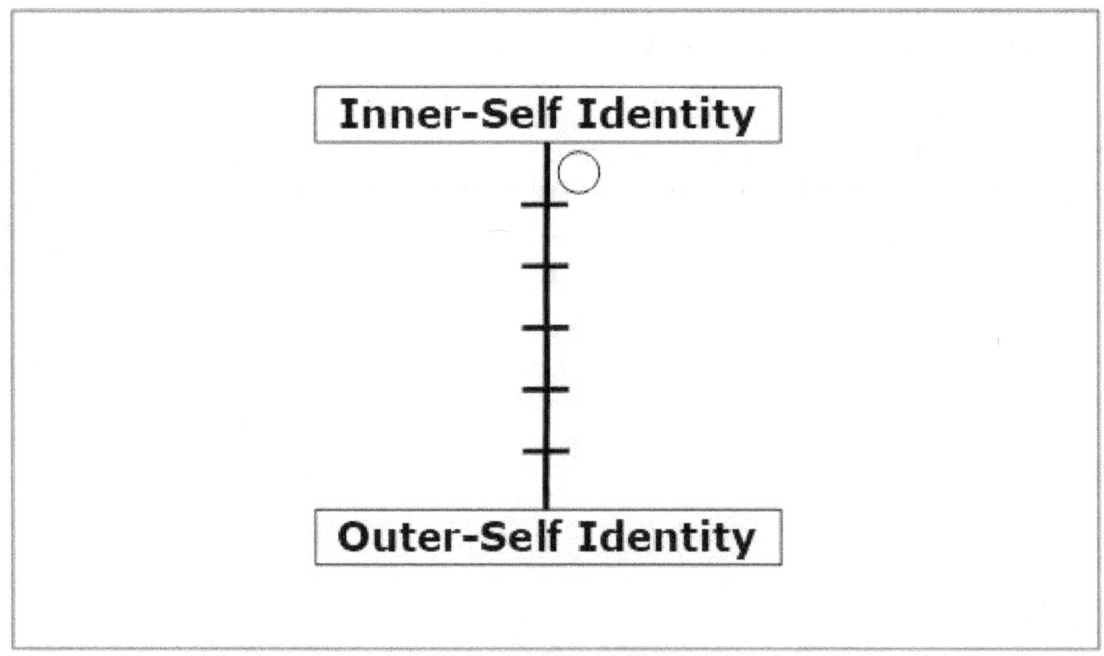

Awareness Level Scale: img 26

We have already covered the motivations, values, emotions, behaviour and perspective or outlook of a character who possesses some level of inner-self-truth-realisation. During the character creation stage, every time you select a truth and a high awareness level in that truth, you are creating part of the character's true inner-self-identity.

Overall Motivations

- o This character will have a continuous flow of inner-self insights forming their interpretations and understanding of experience. Their arguments are usually free of glaring errors

- o Their motivations and values are derived from within themselves and are compatible with all ten inner-self truths

- o Their positive emotional states spring from the alignment of the two selves

- o They have become aware of and are evolving in their true inner-self identity

- o They look for potential rather than comparison

- o Ultimately, the 'Two Selves' of this character are in harmony and this harmony gives rise to their positive personality

- o They look for ways to make the outer environment reflect their inner self truths

Source of the Inner-Self

- o Other names for the inner-self rarely used in this book are consciousness or spirit

- o The inner self of a character comes from a more substantial reality just beyond the reaches of the character's physical senses

- o The inner self of a character has a purpose, and that purpose is to evolve.

   Its purpose is to realise and to develop itself fully in terms of the ten truths covered in this book.

   This inner-self is the true identity of a character

- o The inner self of a character logs into the physical world via the physical infant

- o The inner-self and its purpose are first in order. It exists before its outer-self and its outer-self experiences.

   These experiences are intended to aid the character's inner-self purpose to evolve in all truths

- o A character having a high awareness level of their inner-self will have motivations, values, emotions, behaviour, and perspective based in the truths of their inner-self

- o A character who has realised their authentic inner-self-identity lives within their all-possibility inner-self and attempts to bring those inner-self truths to their outer-self identity

Outer-Self Identity

Have a look at the following image:

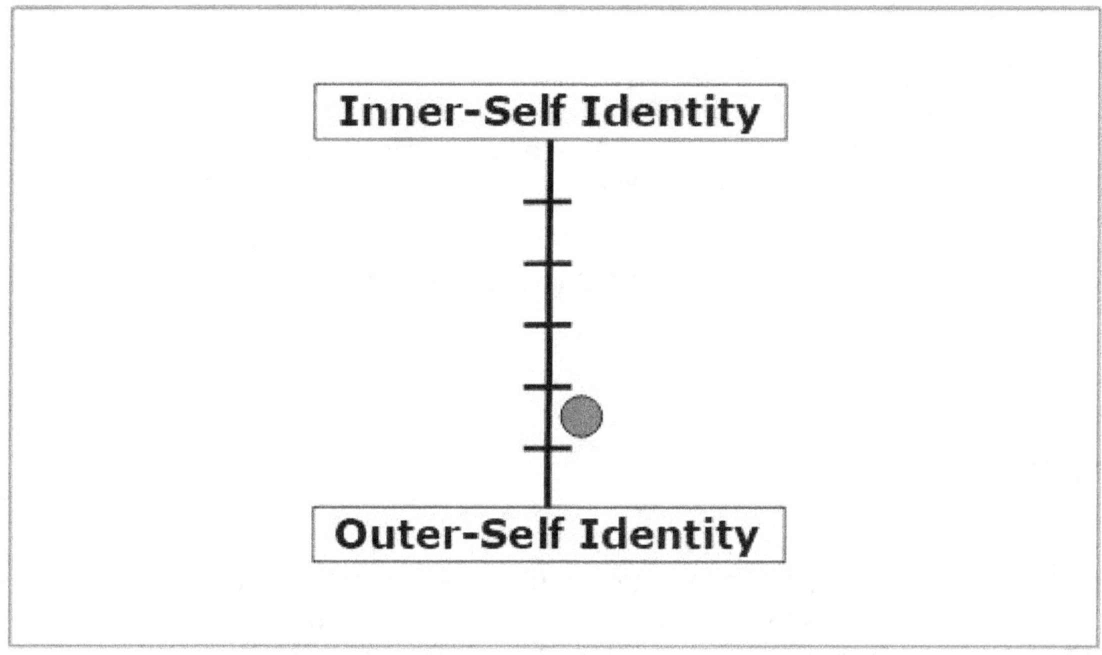

Awareness Level Scale: img 27

We have also covered what the motivations, values, emotions, behaviour and perspective or outlook of a character will be who possess little or no awareness of their inner self truths. They have no choice but to believe they are the extremely limited outer-self-identity.

Again, during the character creation stage, every time you select a truth and a low awareness level for a given character in that truth, you are creating part of their mainly blind and limited outer-self-identity.

Overall Motivations

- o This character will only have their outer-self interpretations and understanding of experience.

  Their interpretations, without the guidance of their inner-self truths, are bound to be full of errors

- o Their motivations and values are derived solely from their outer-self world and are usually incompatible with all ten of their inner-self truths

- o Their negative emotional states spring from the non-alignment between the two selves

- o This character remains unaware of their true inner-self identity

- o They always look at comparisons rather than potential

- o Ultimately, the 'Two Selves' of this character are in conflict and that conflict gives rise to their negative personality

- o This character tends to reflect the environment in their perspective and behaviour

Source of the Outer-Self

- o Contrary to the science within a character's outer-self world, which says that they have an upward evolution - rising out of a soup of molecules to their present conscious awareness - a character's physical outer-self is derived from an outward evolution

- o The inner-self of a character outwardly creates the physical outer-self of the character across their life from conception to infancy to old-age

- o The outer-identity of a character is a social identity derived from interactions with the society they exist in

- o The truths of the inner self of a character are always present, but hidden below the character's conscious awareness.

  As the character goes through the mill of experience, those hidden truths are released slowly to their awareness and interpretations.

  In this gradual way, they fulfil their purpose to evolve.

  But the outer-self social identity purposes of a character block that release or slow it down

- o The more extensive system from which the true inner-self-identity of the character belongs is first in order, while the outer-self social identity of a character and their society is second in order.

  But the outer-self focused character puts all emphasis on his outer-self identity

- o The character's outer-self purpose should also be second to their inner-self purpose.

  But an outer-self focused character will always put their outer-self purpose first in order

- A character's motivations, values, emotions, behaviour, and their perspective should begin with the inner-self, and not with the outer-self and their society

- Having not realised their true inner-self-identity, they live outside of themselves as the extremely limited and suffering outer-self-identity.